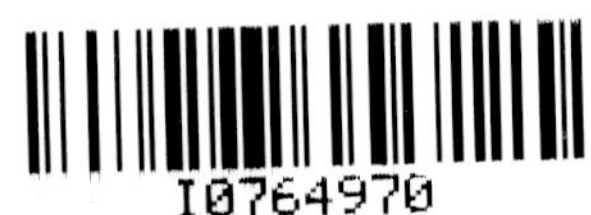

The Book of 35 Lion Images Stress Relieving Designs for Adults & Kids Relaxation

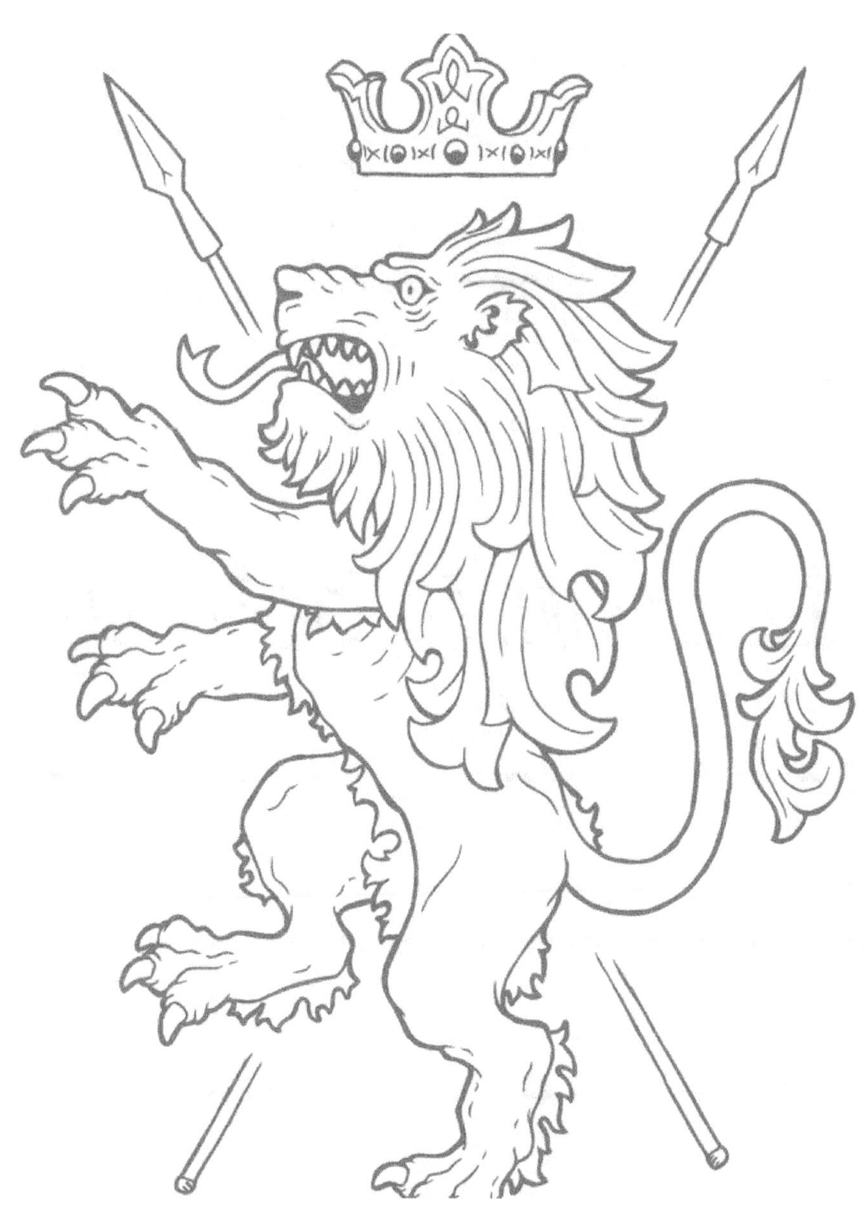

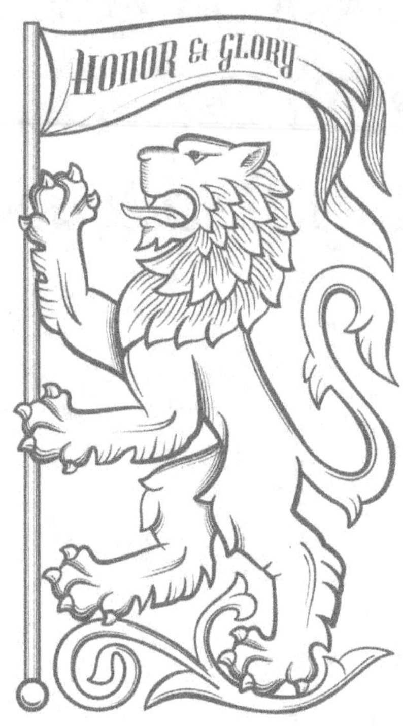

This book is belong to

____

____

____

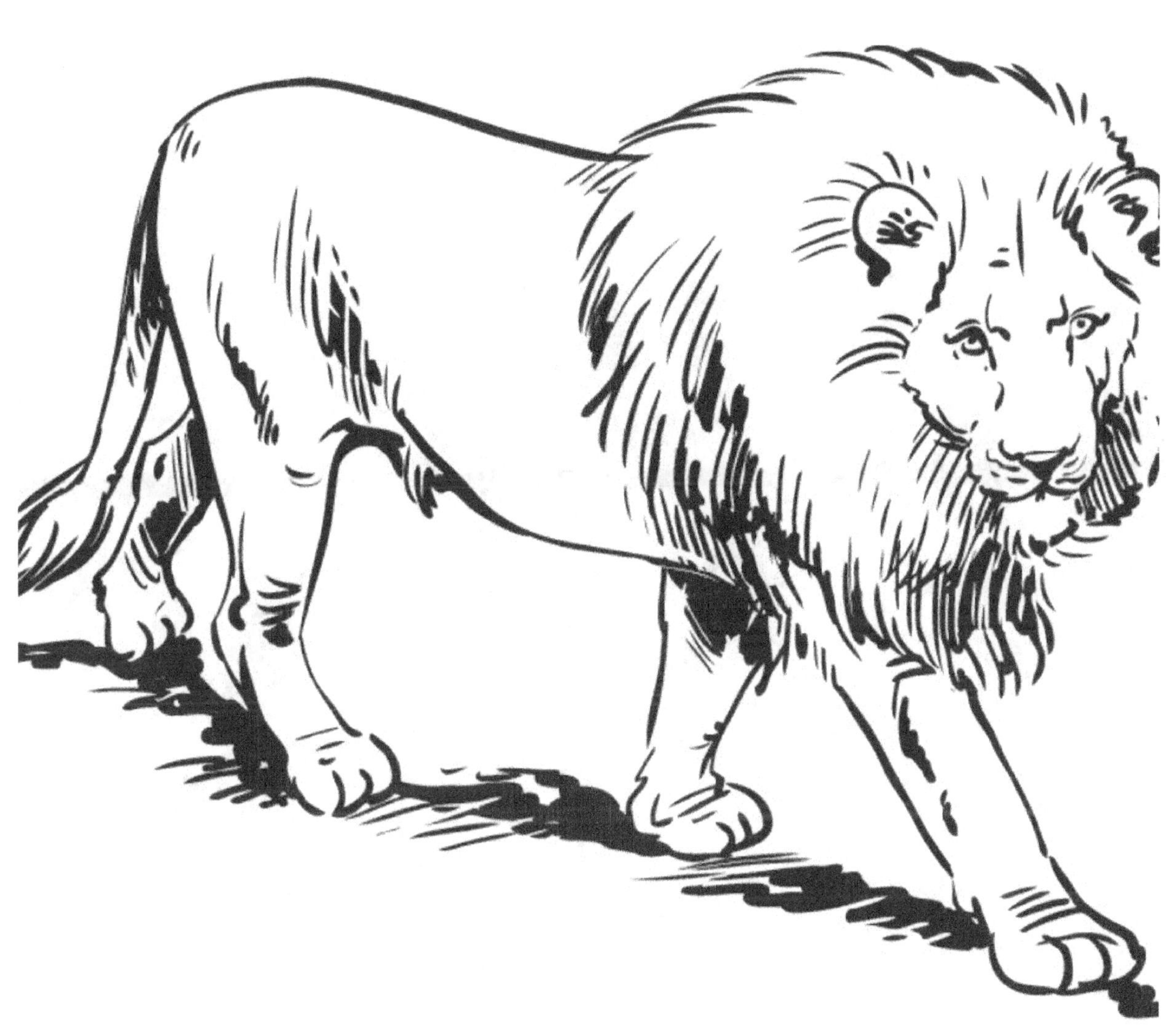

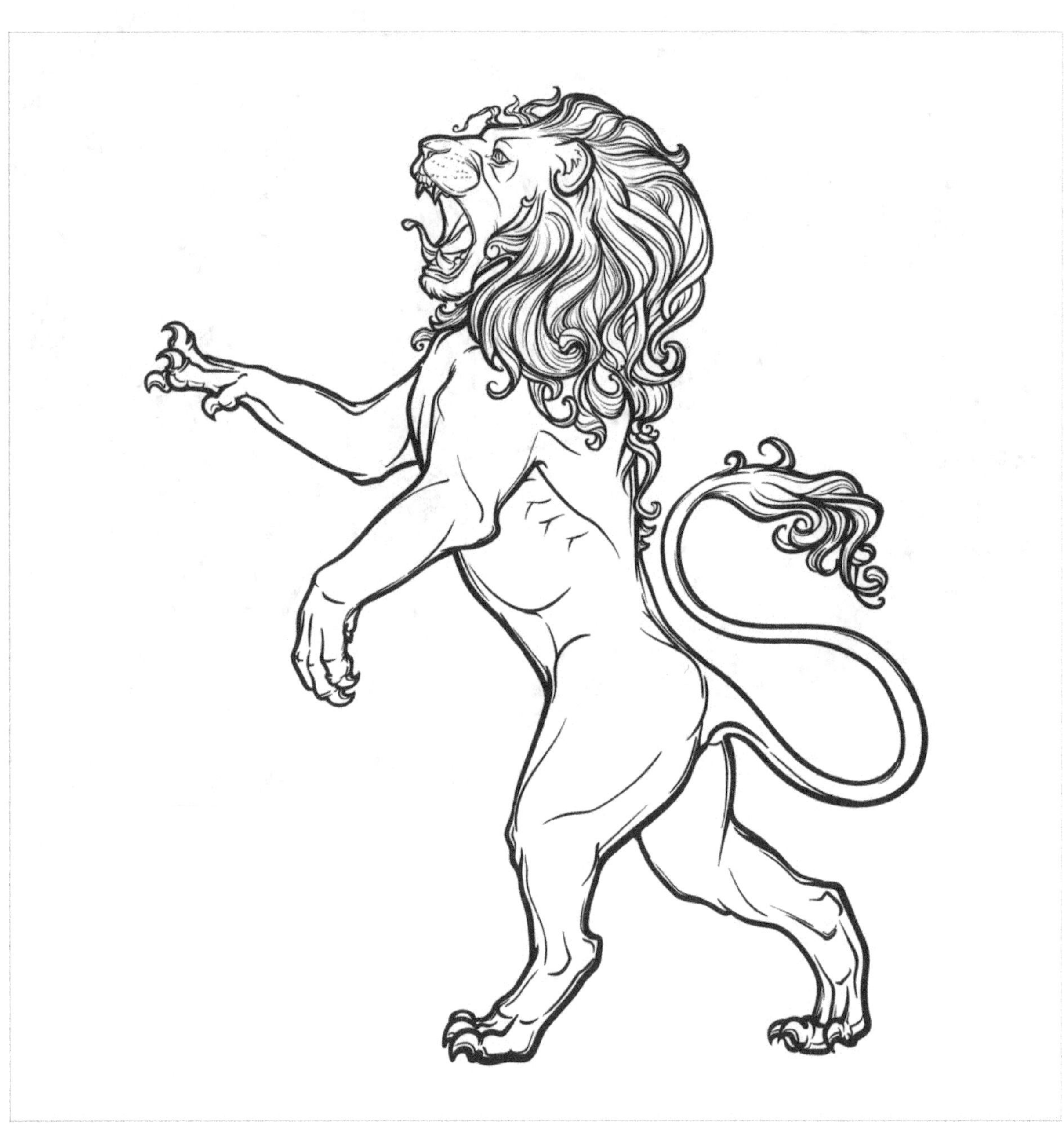

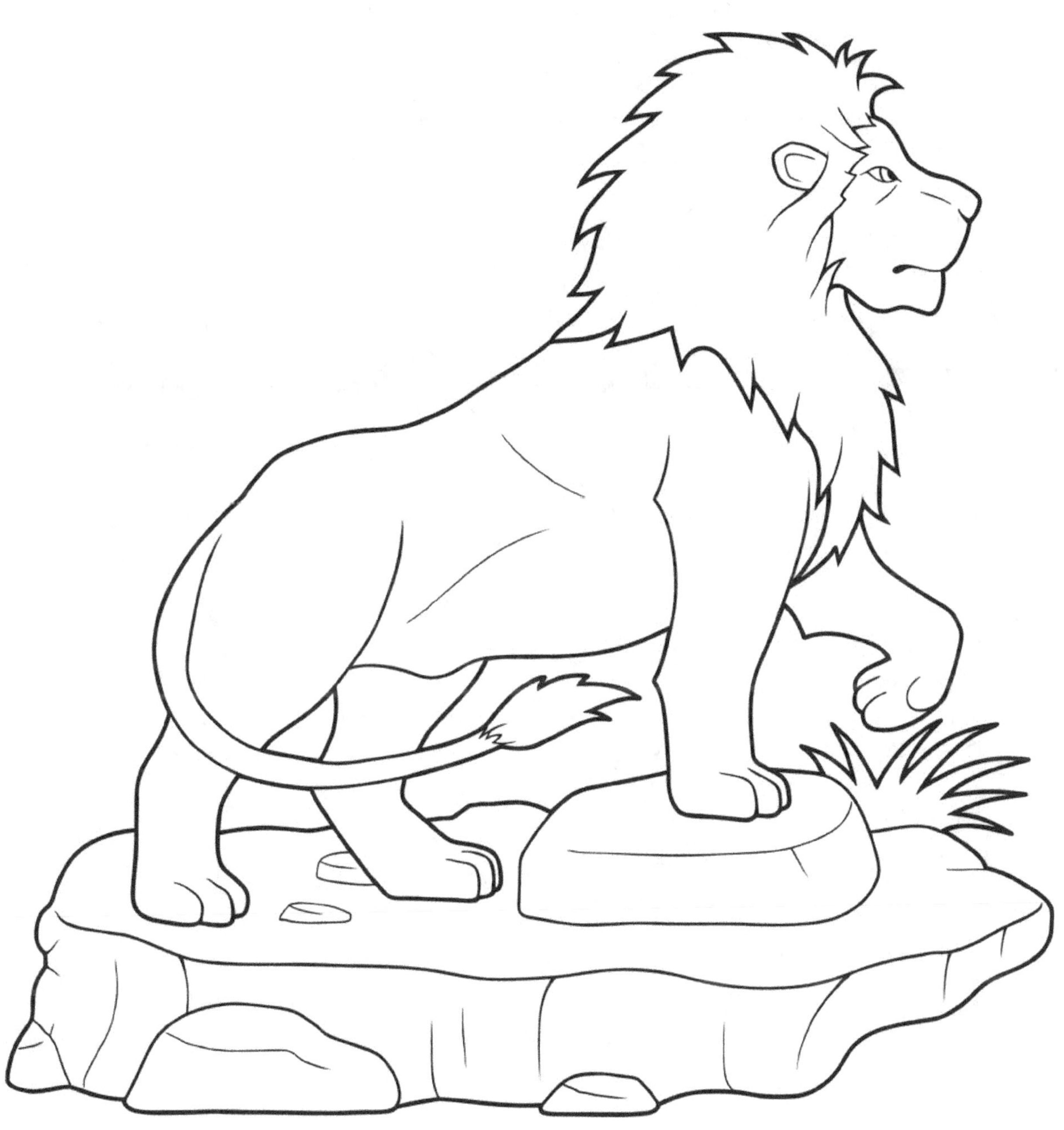

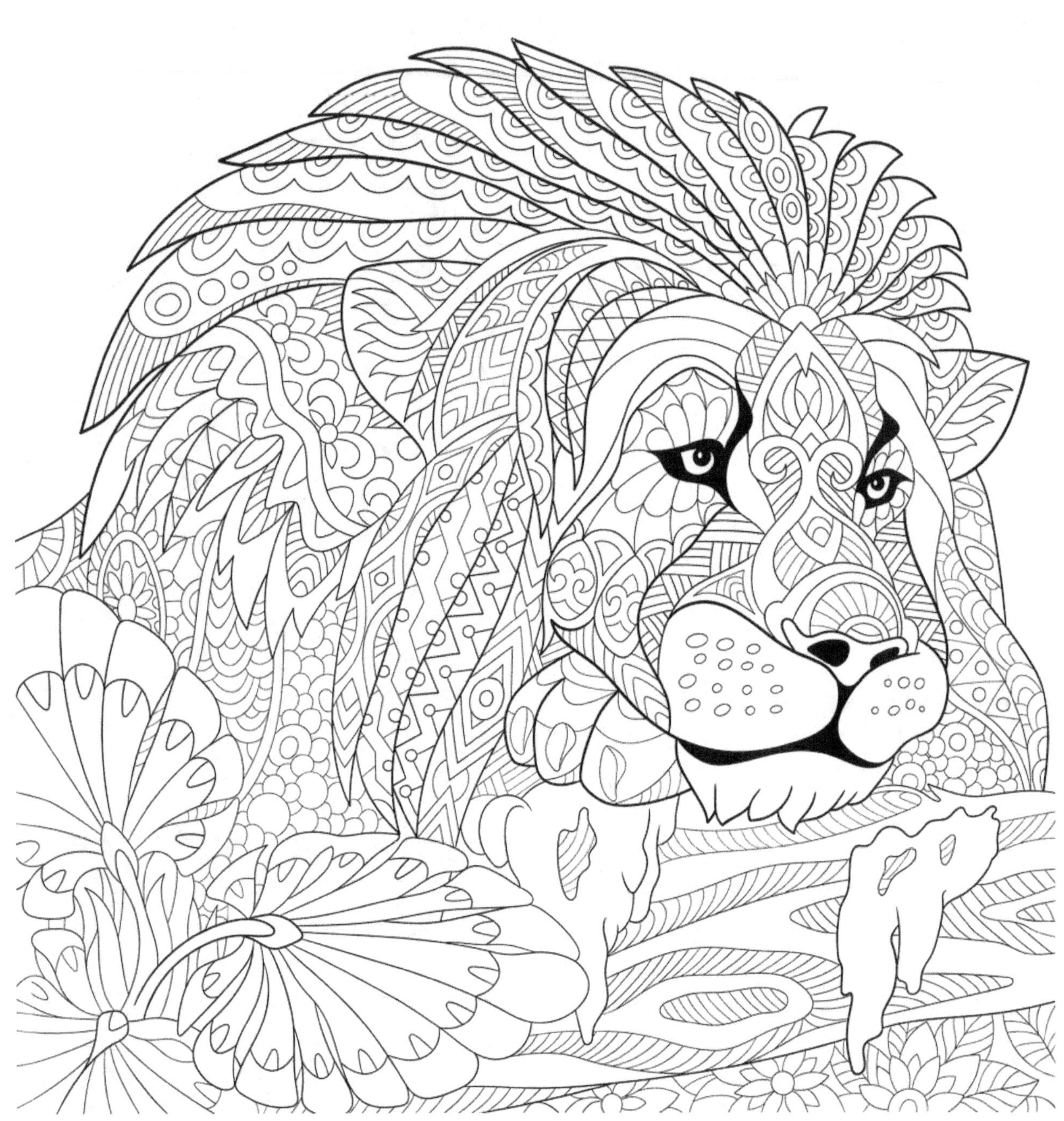

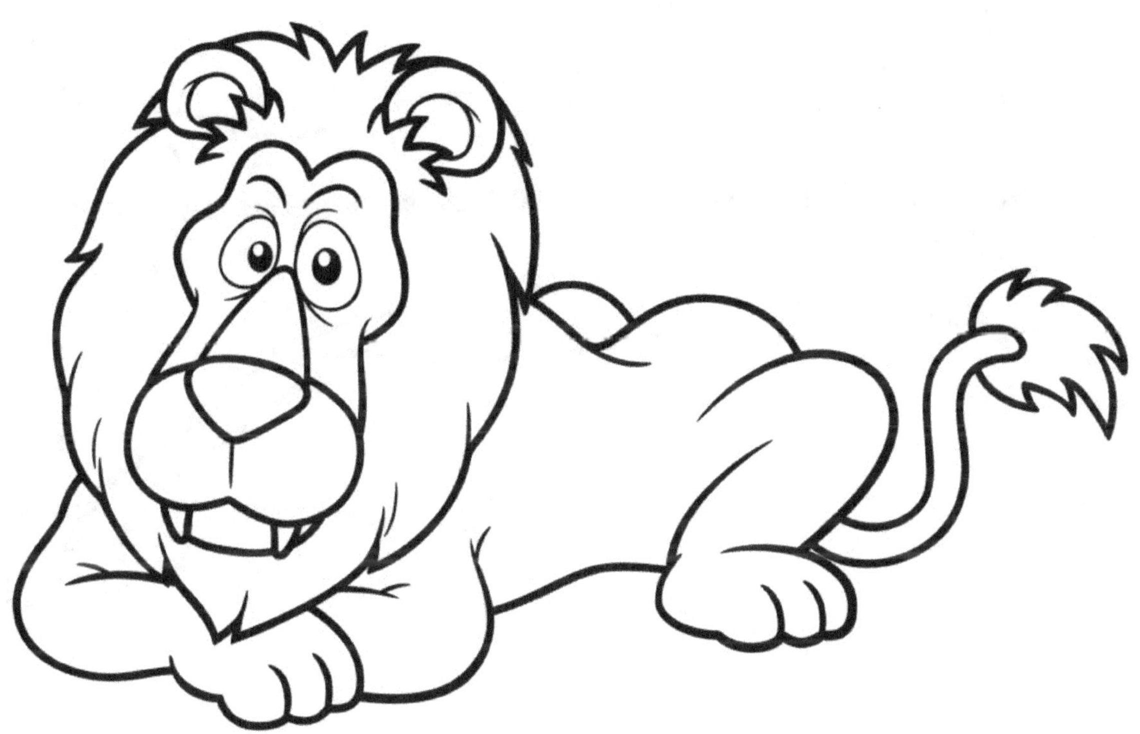

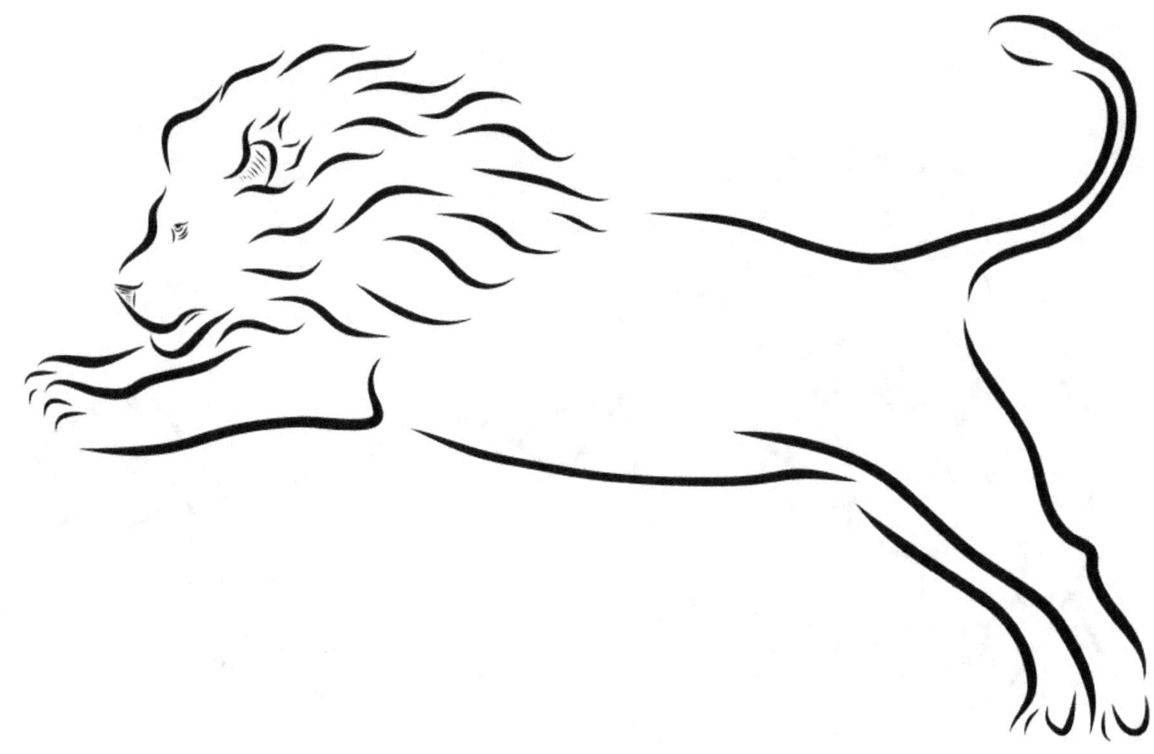

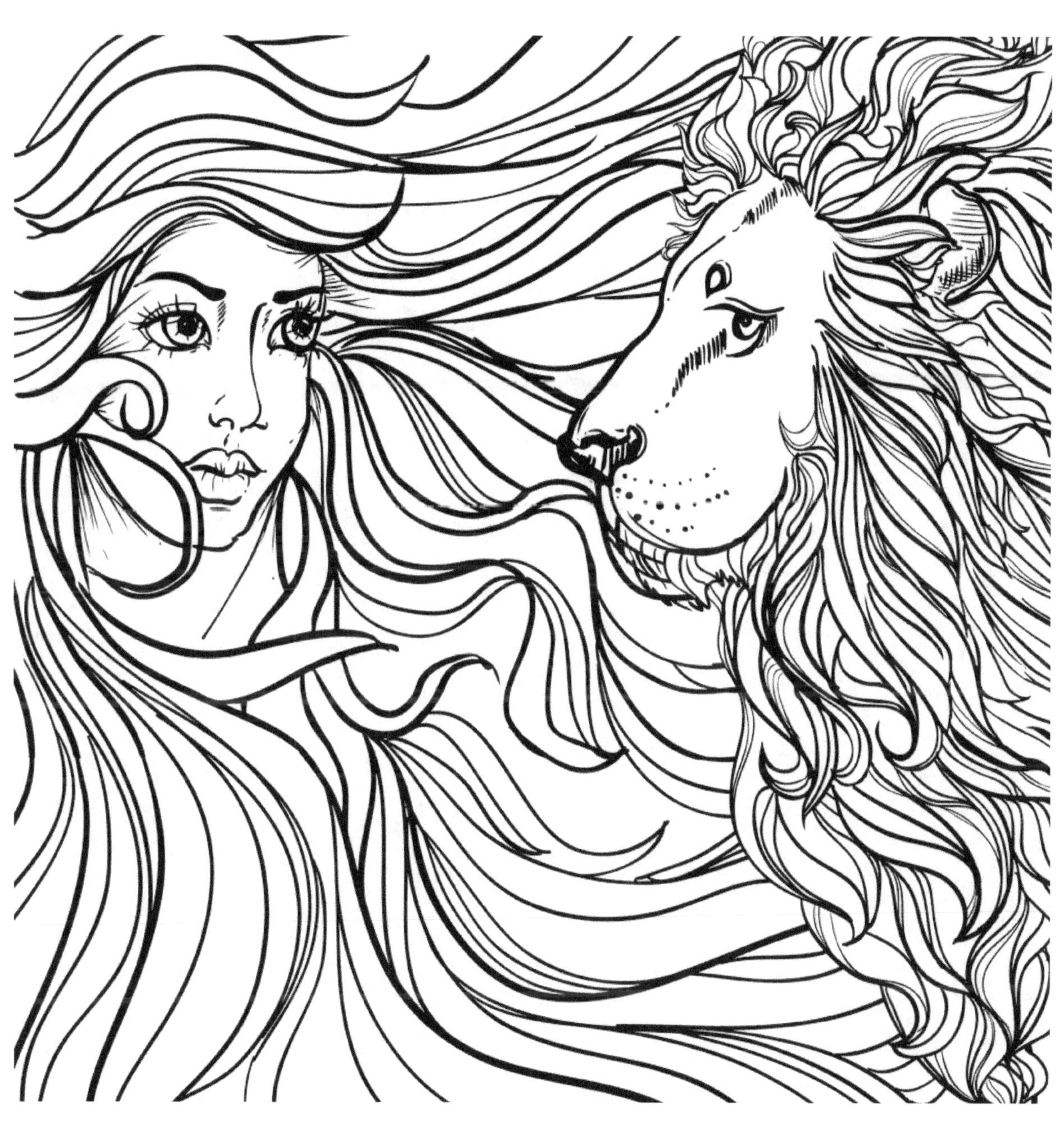

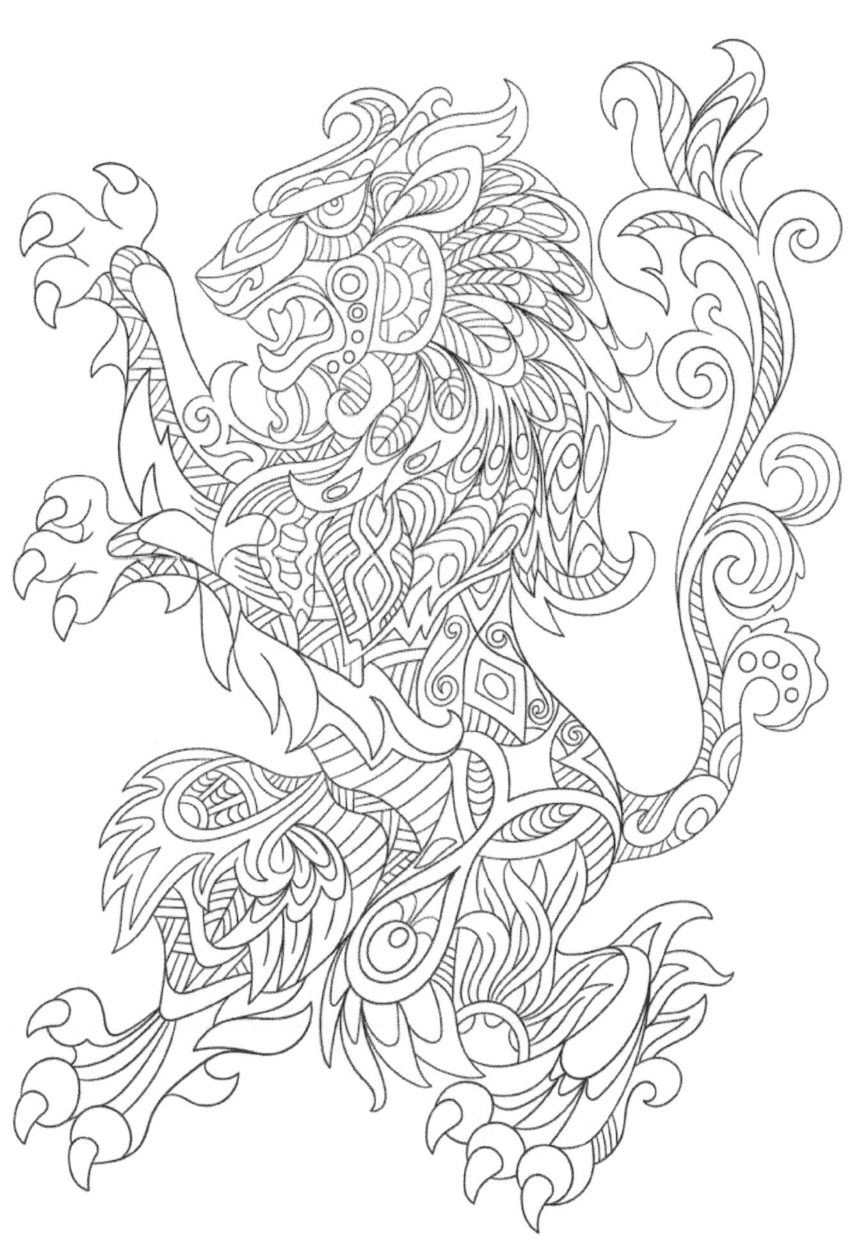

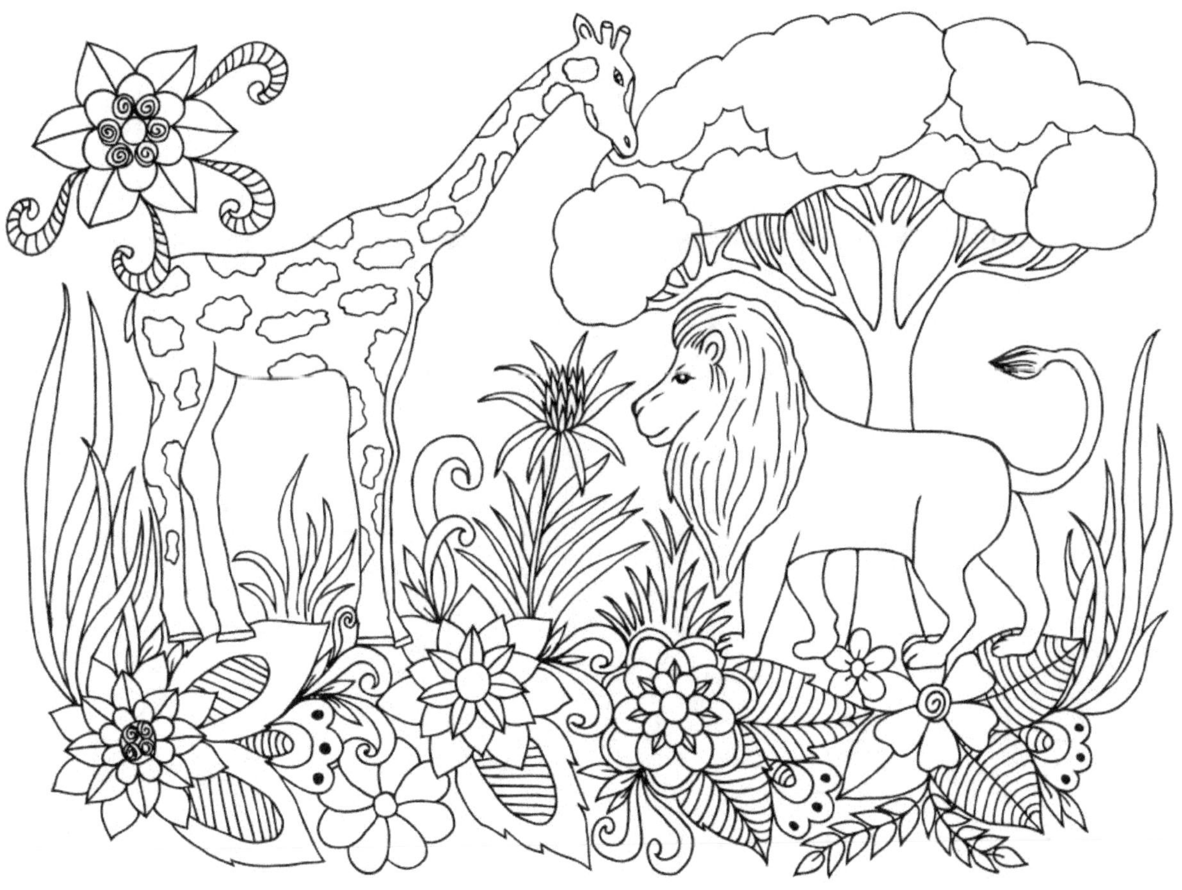

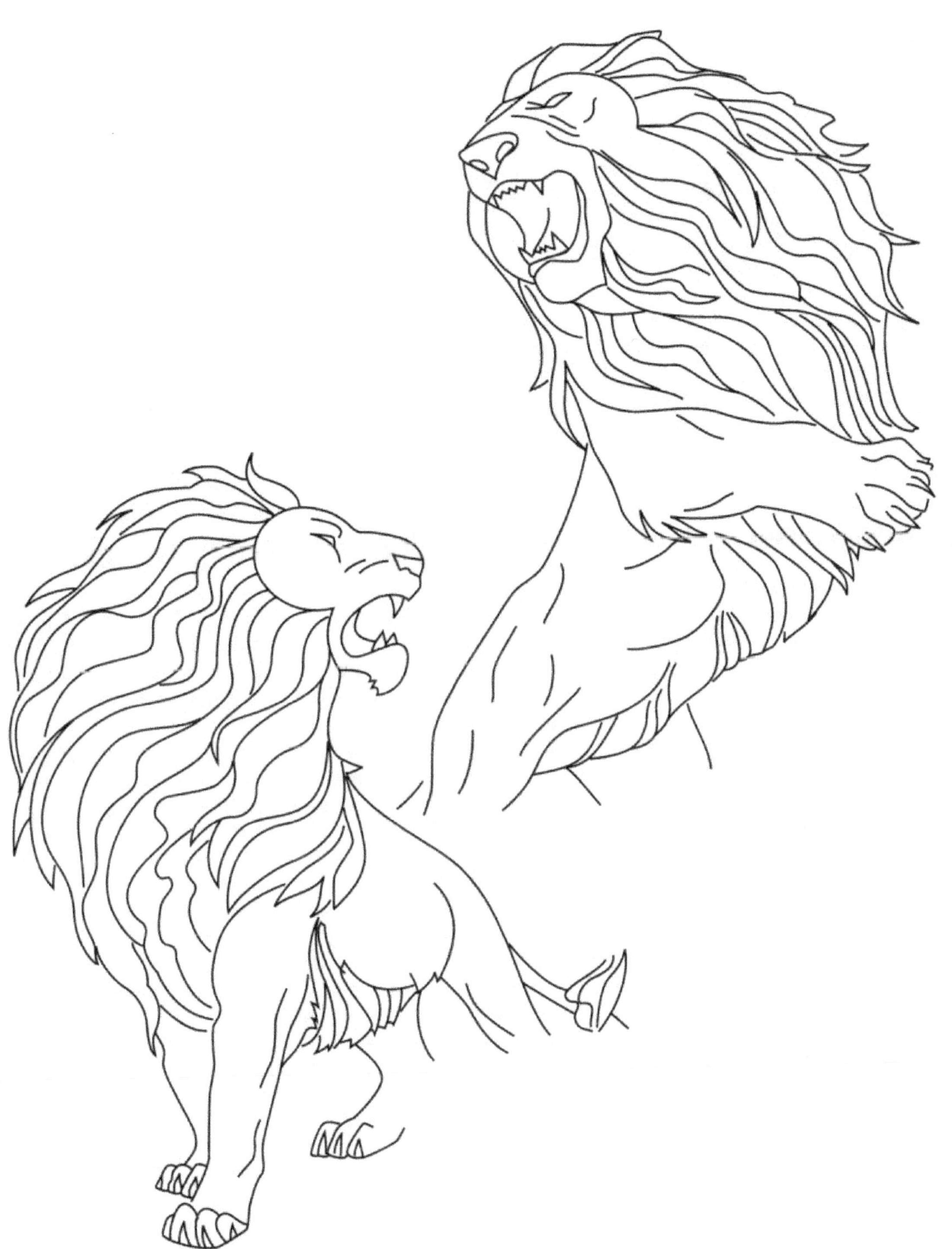

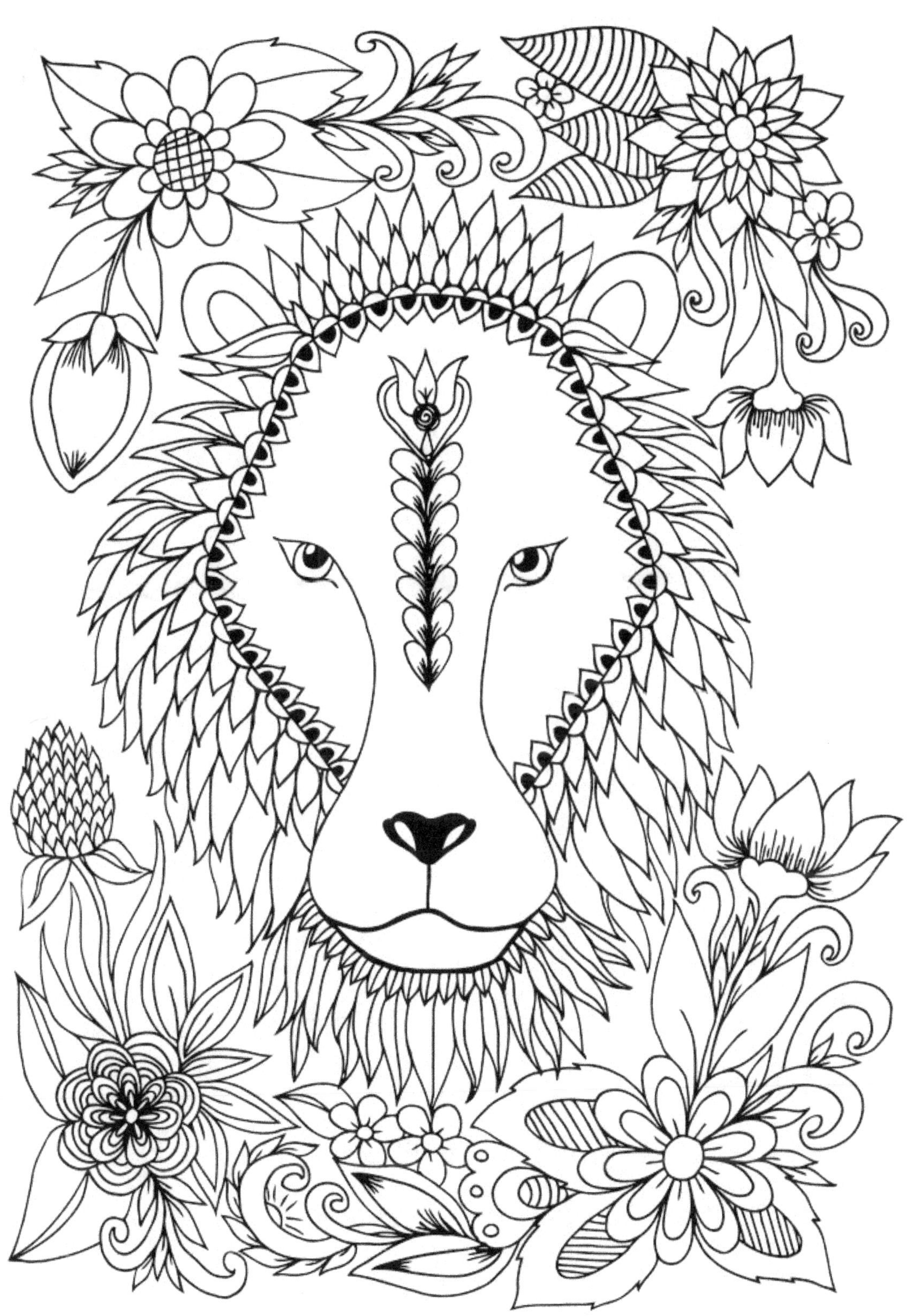

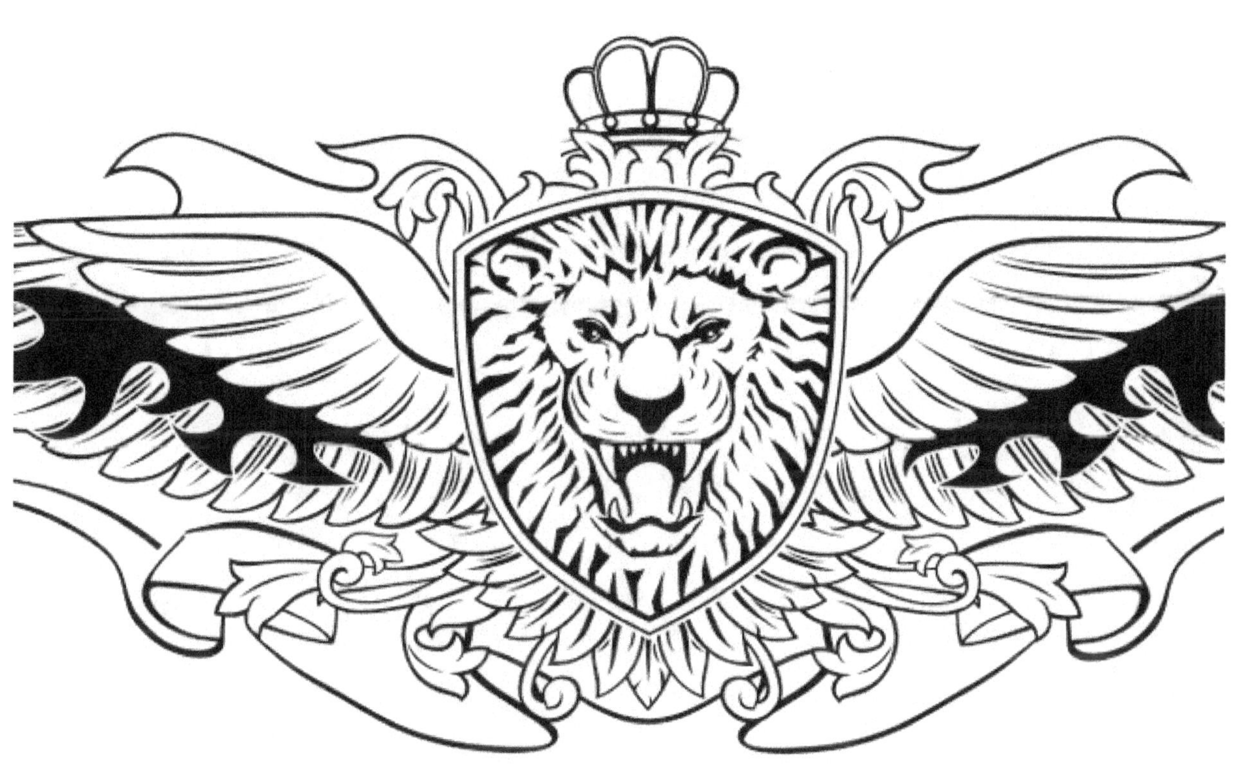

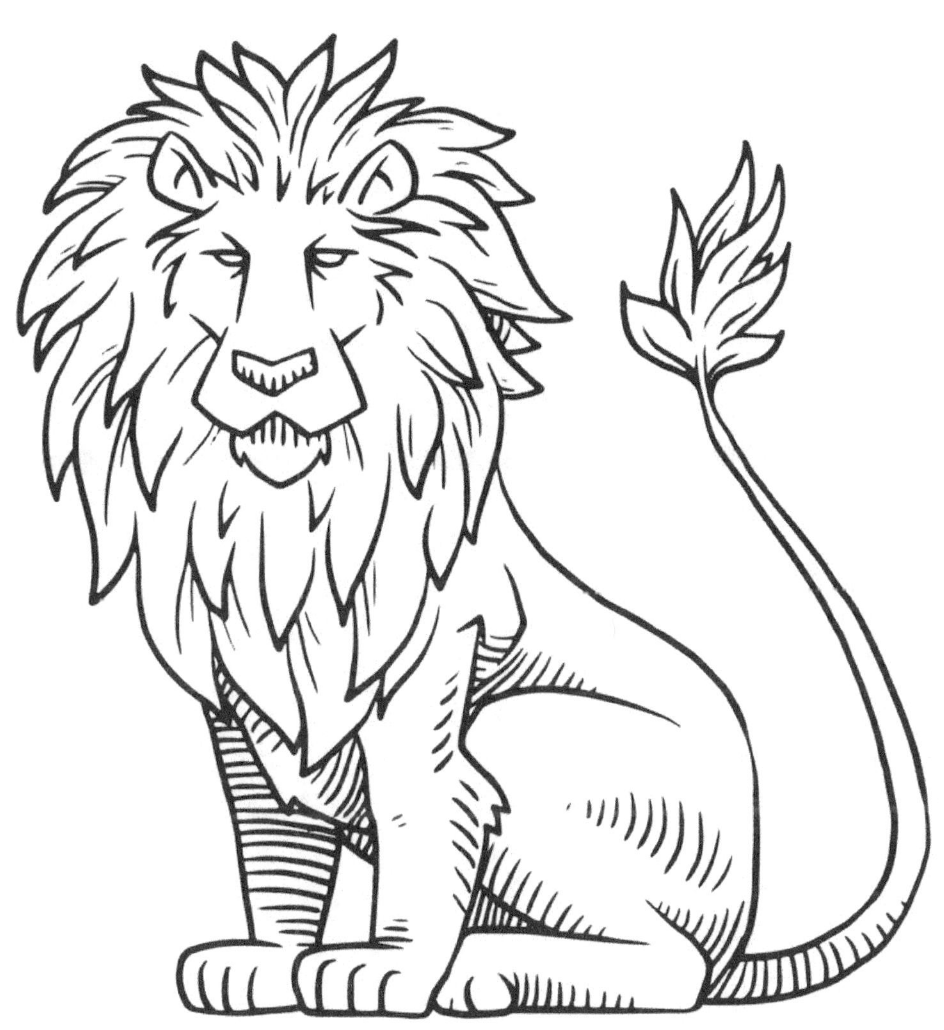

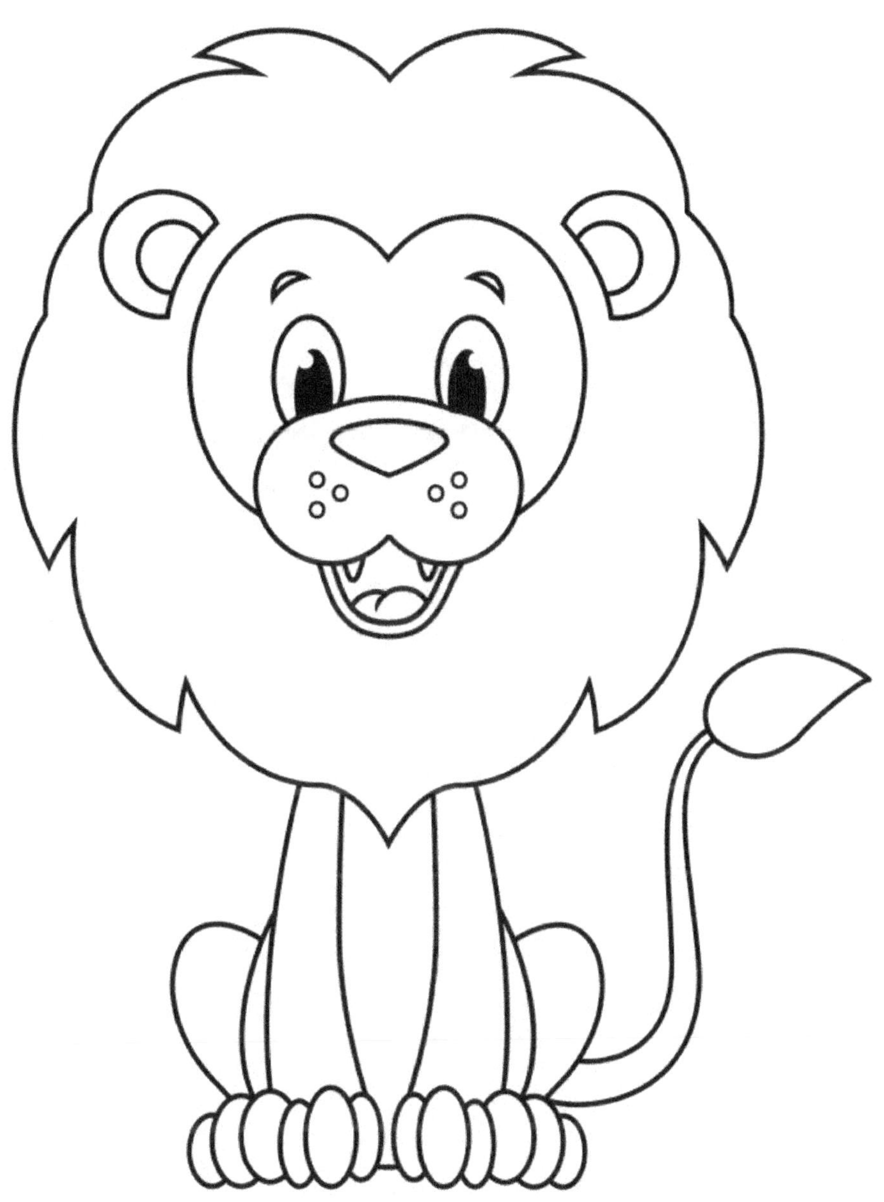

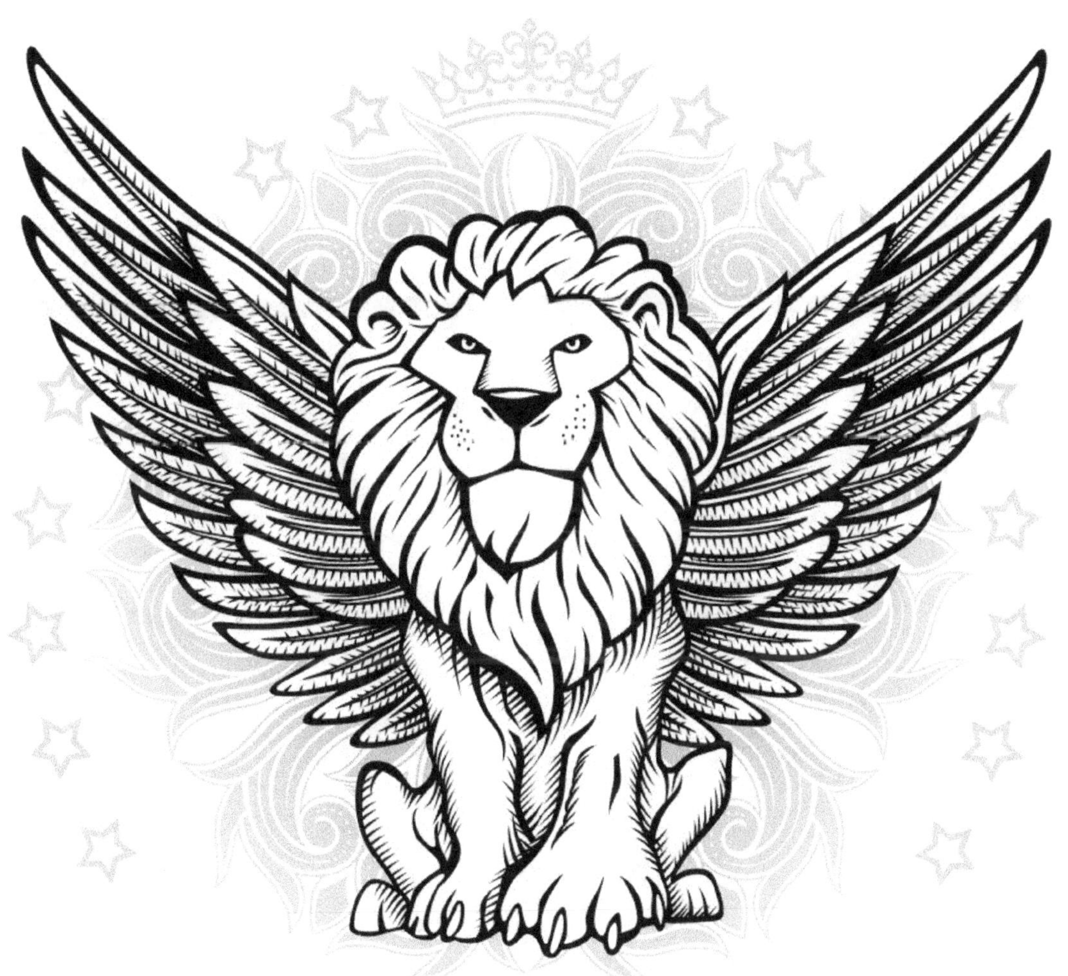

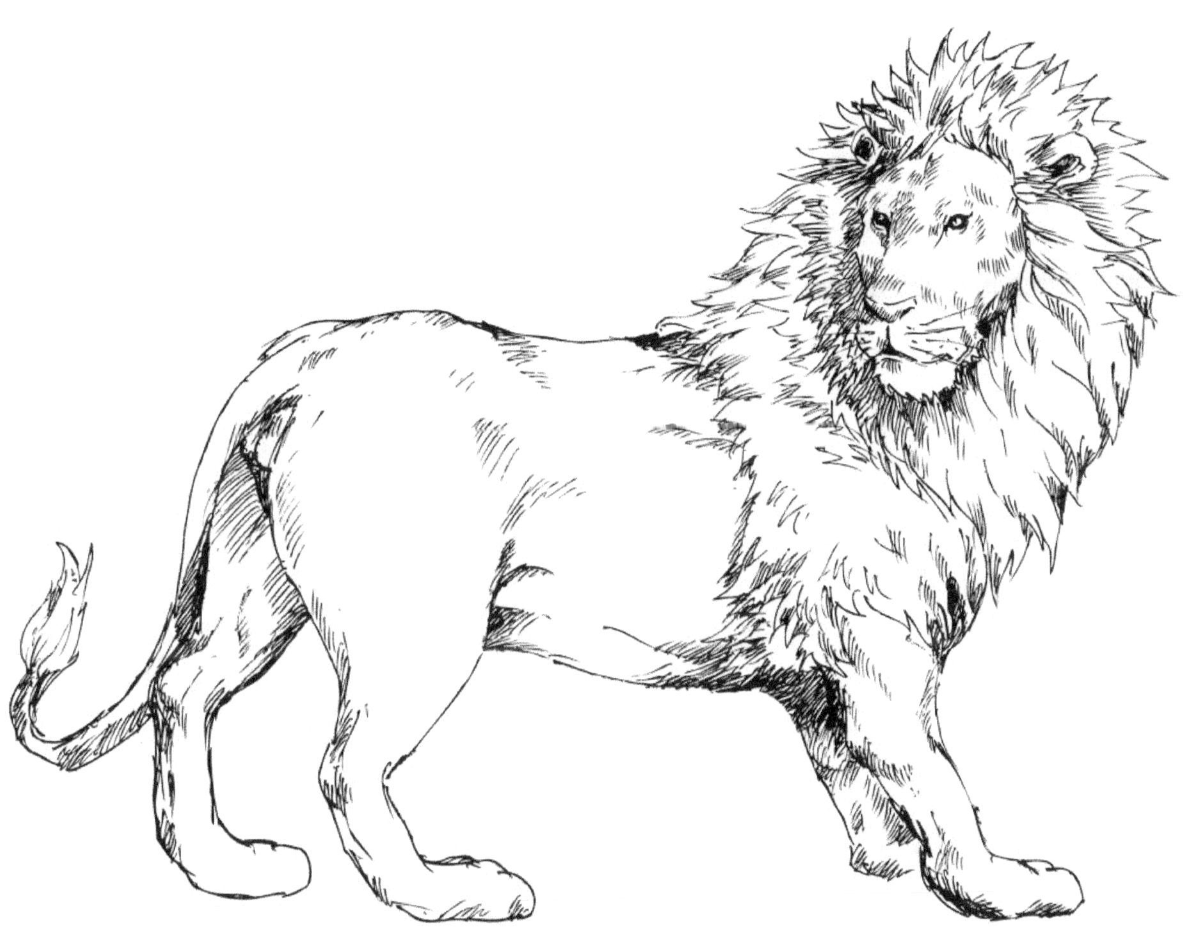

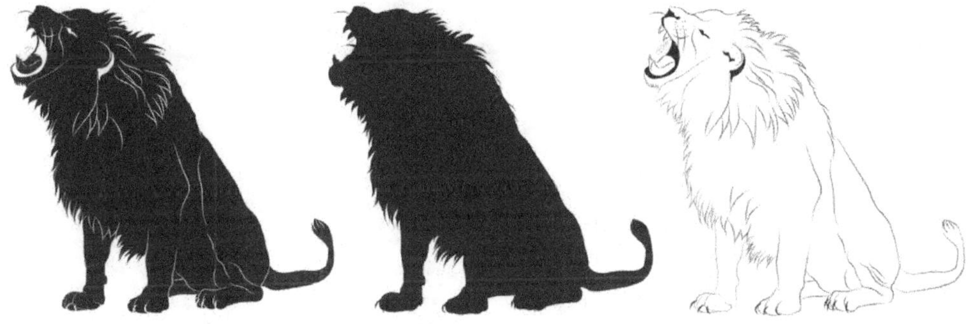

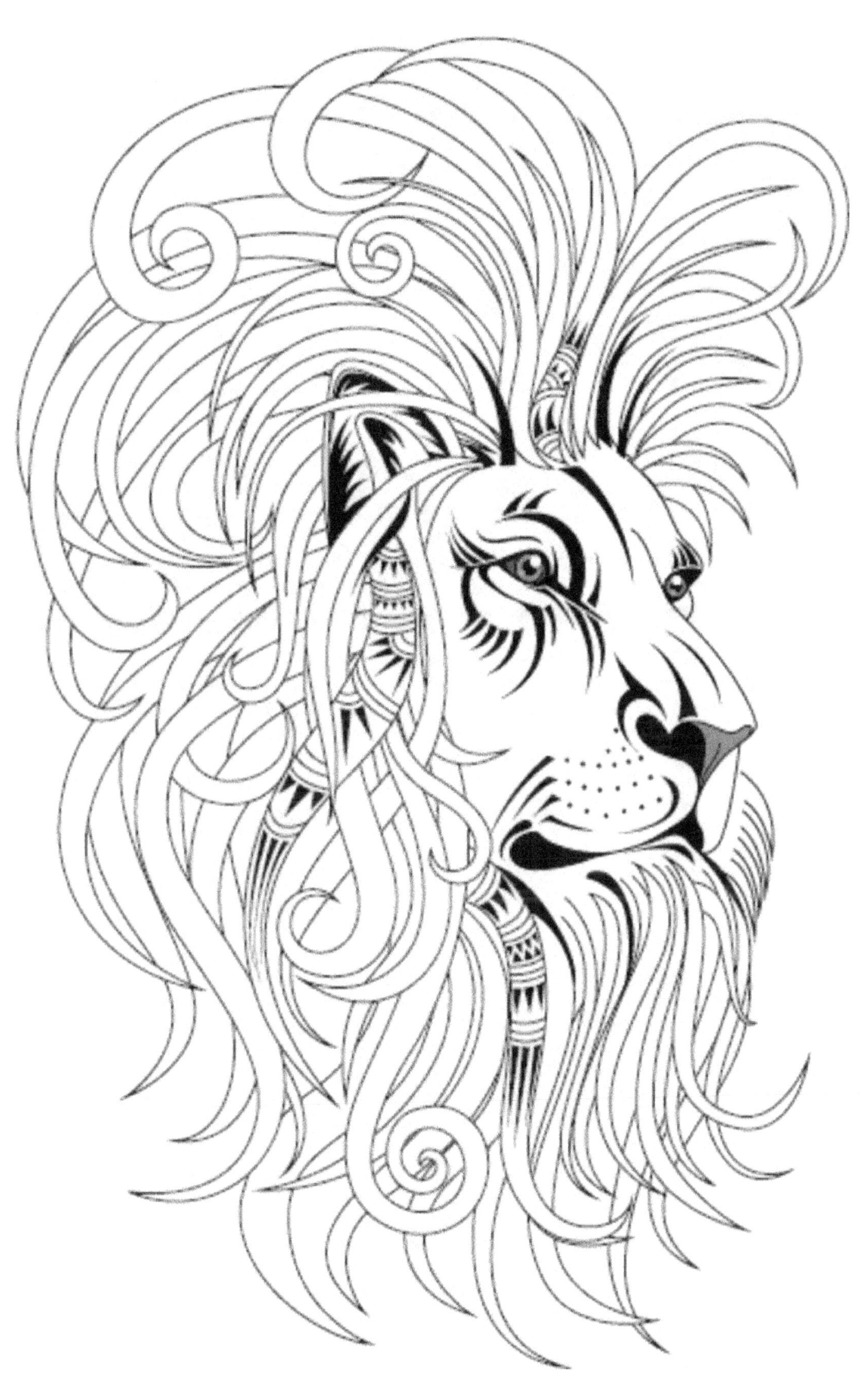

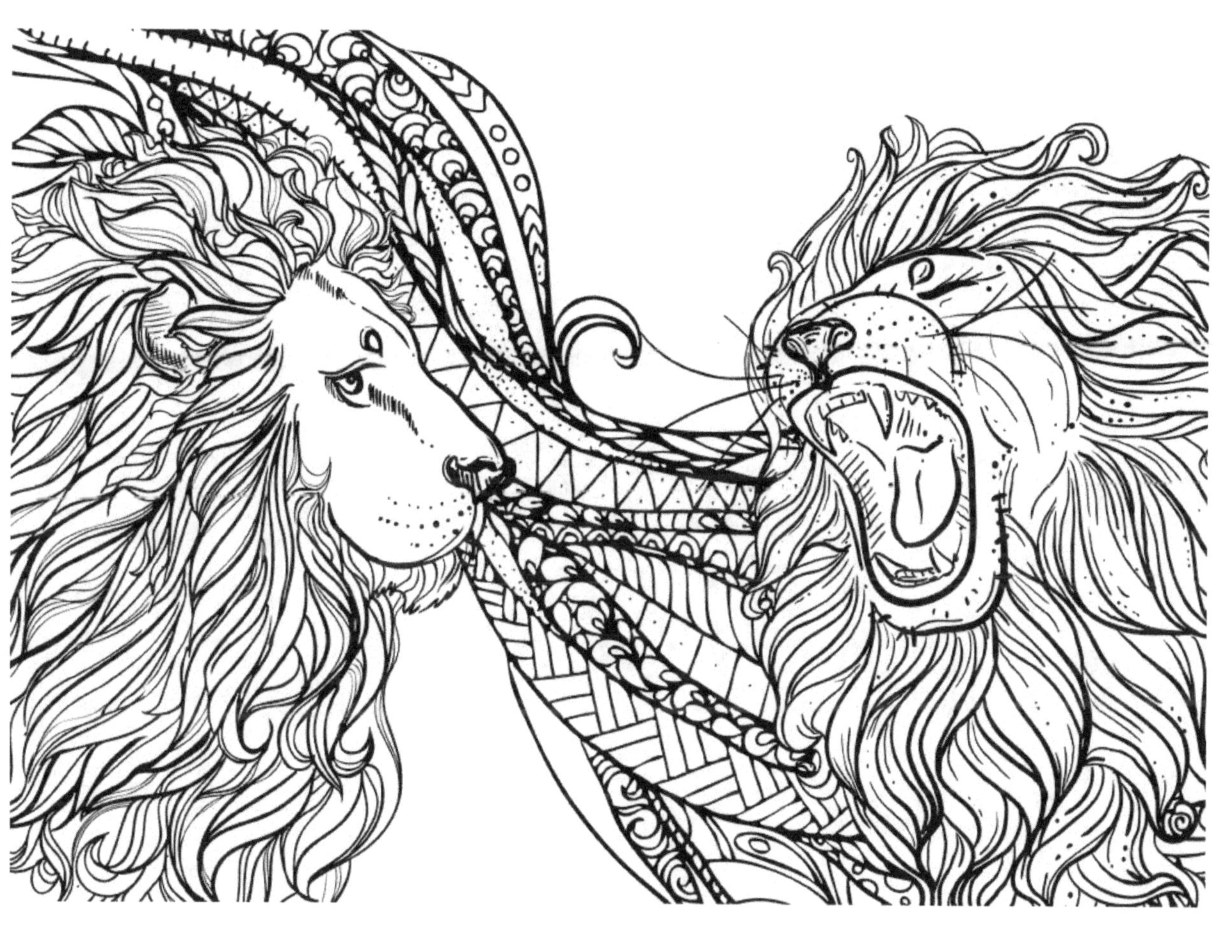

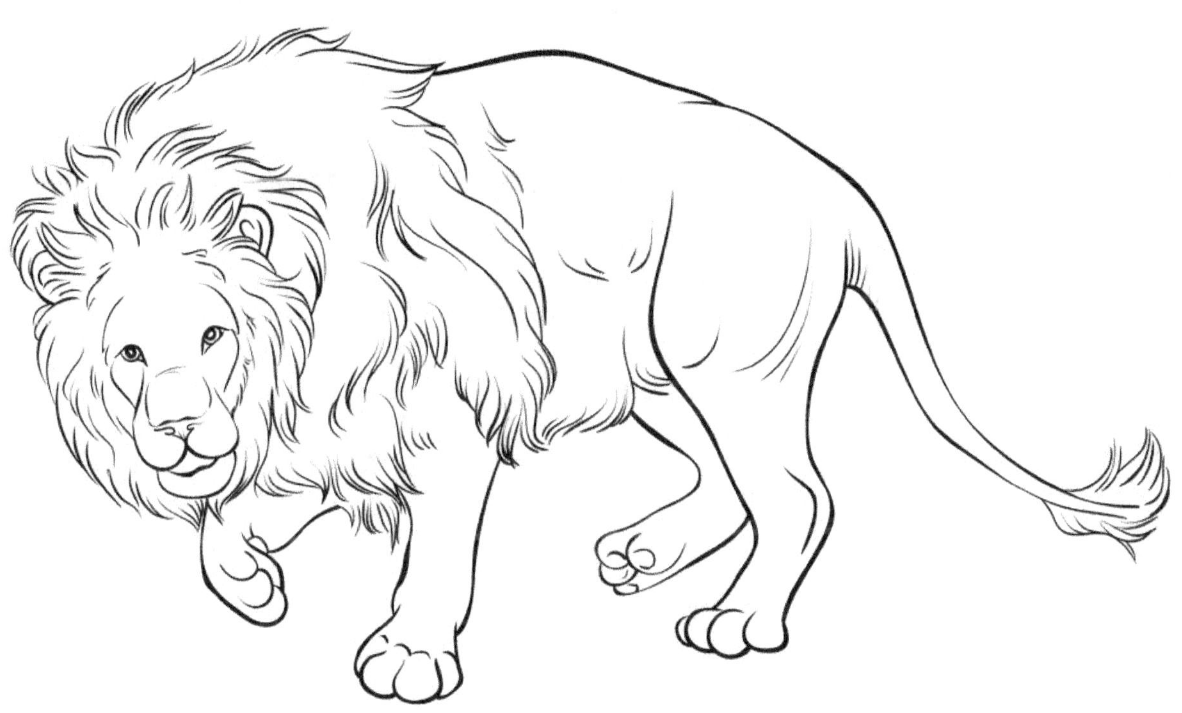

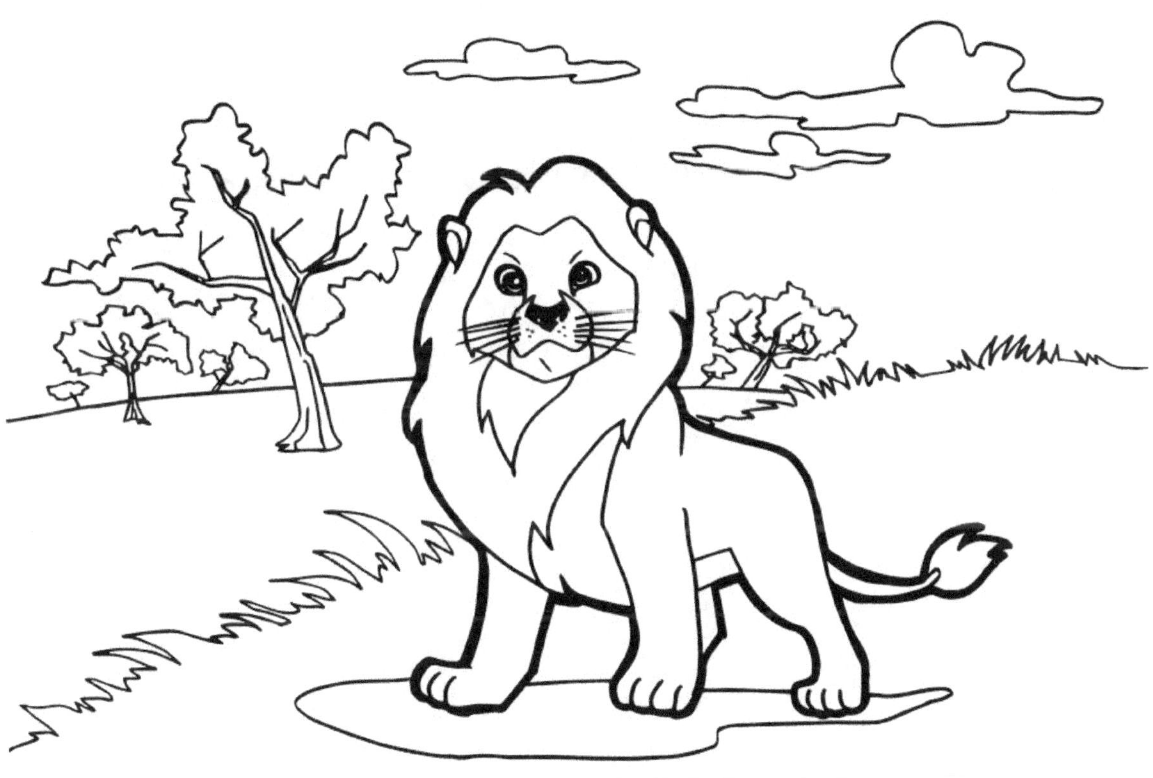

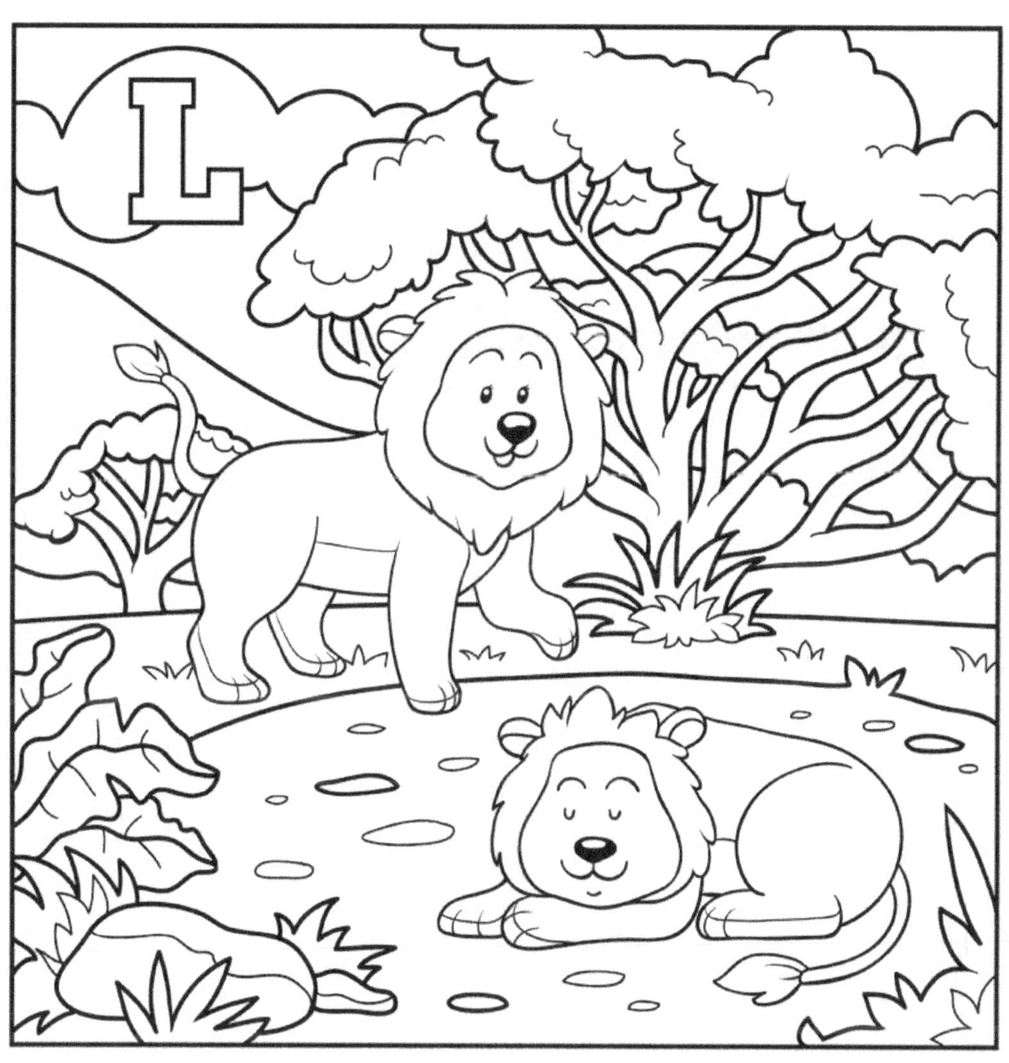

L

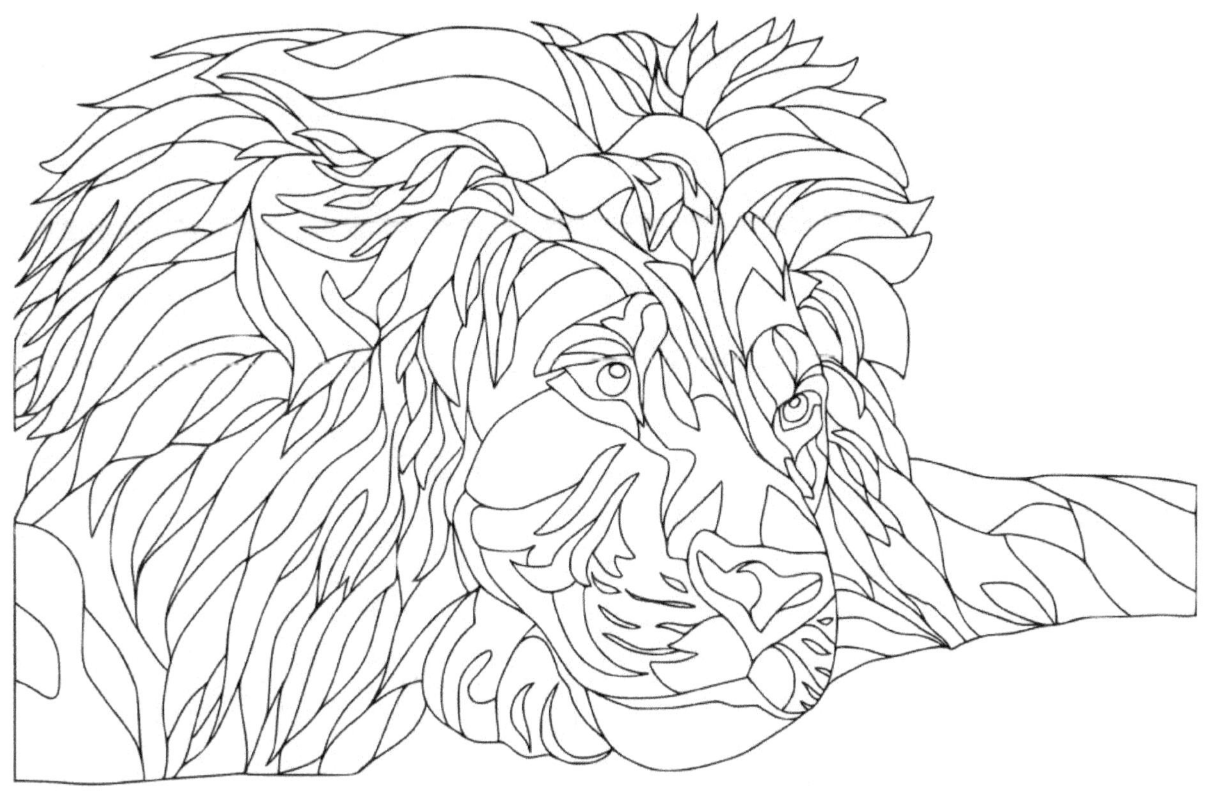

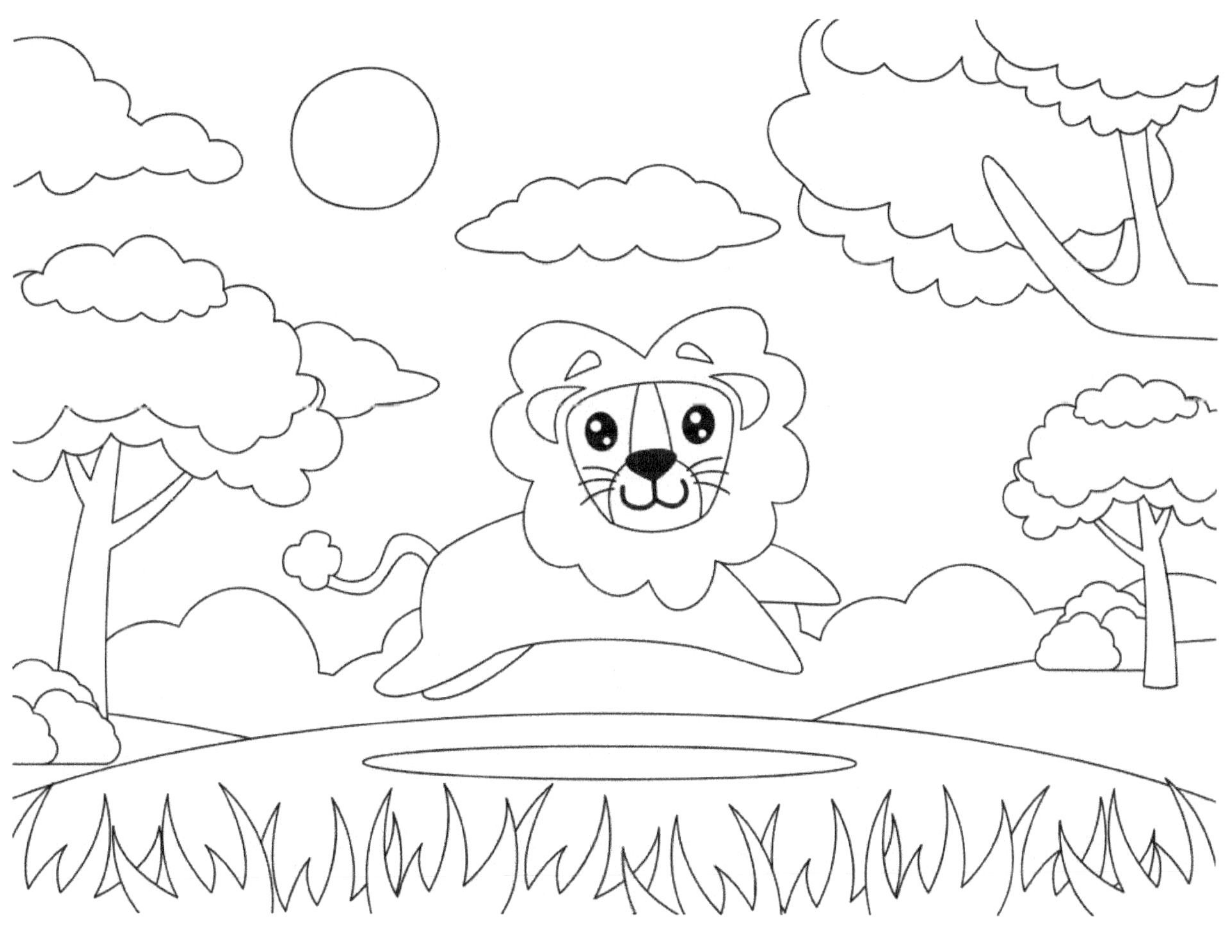

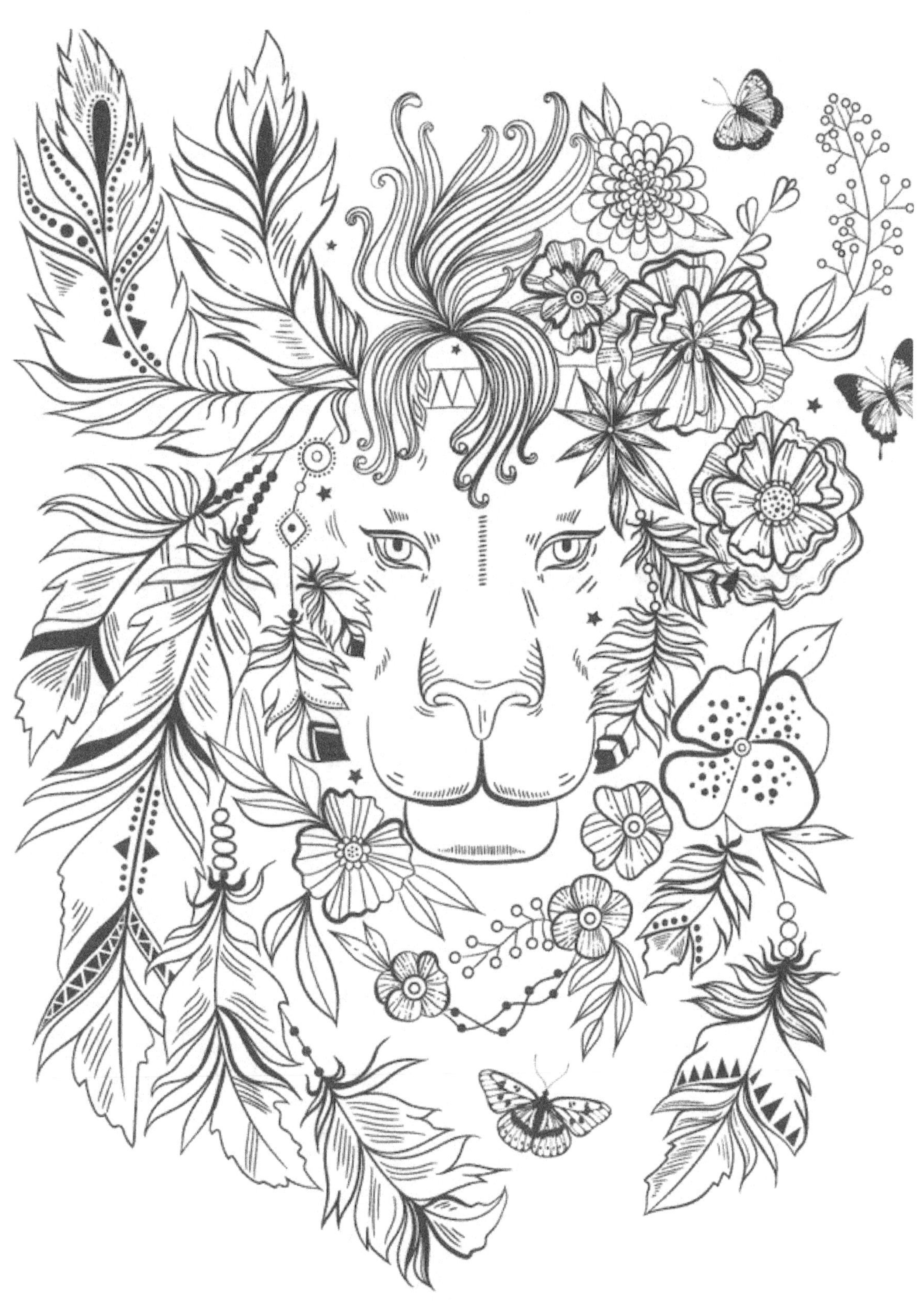

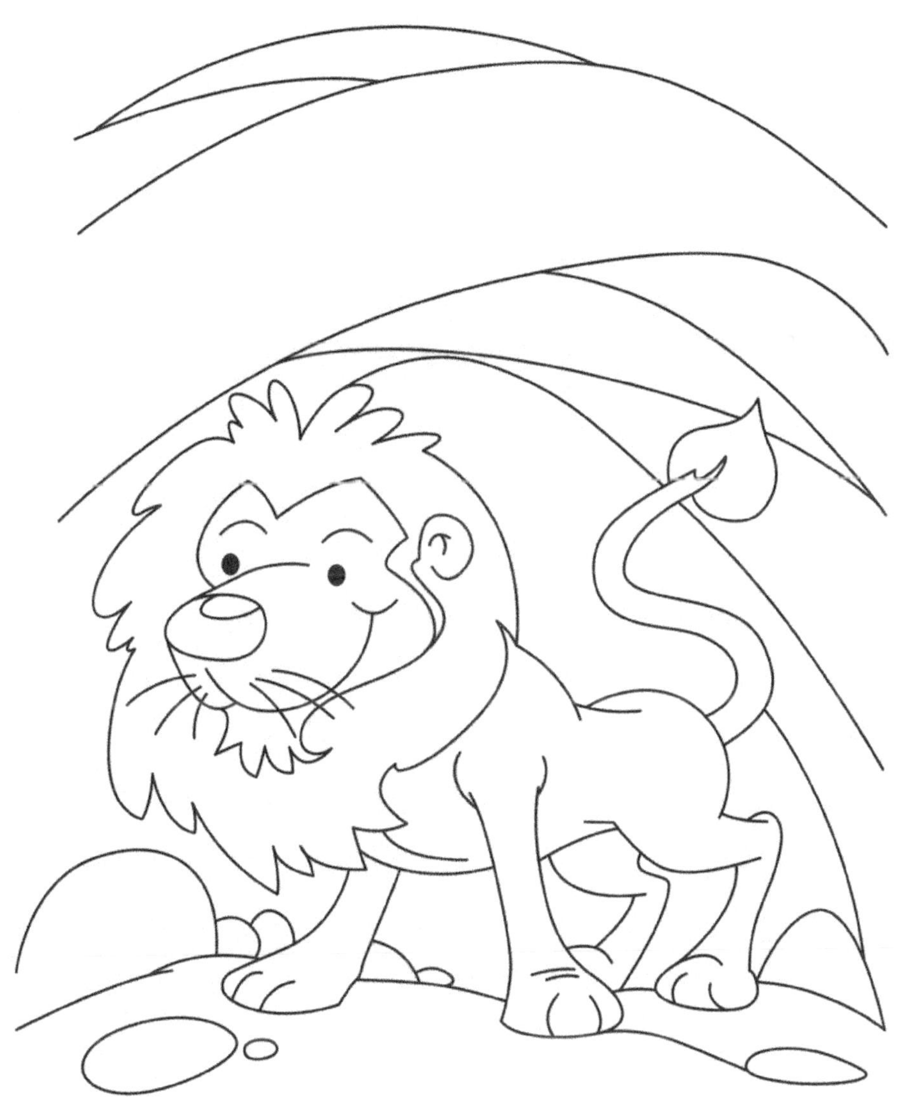

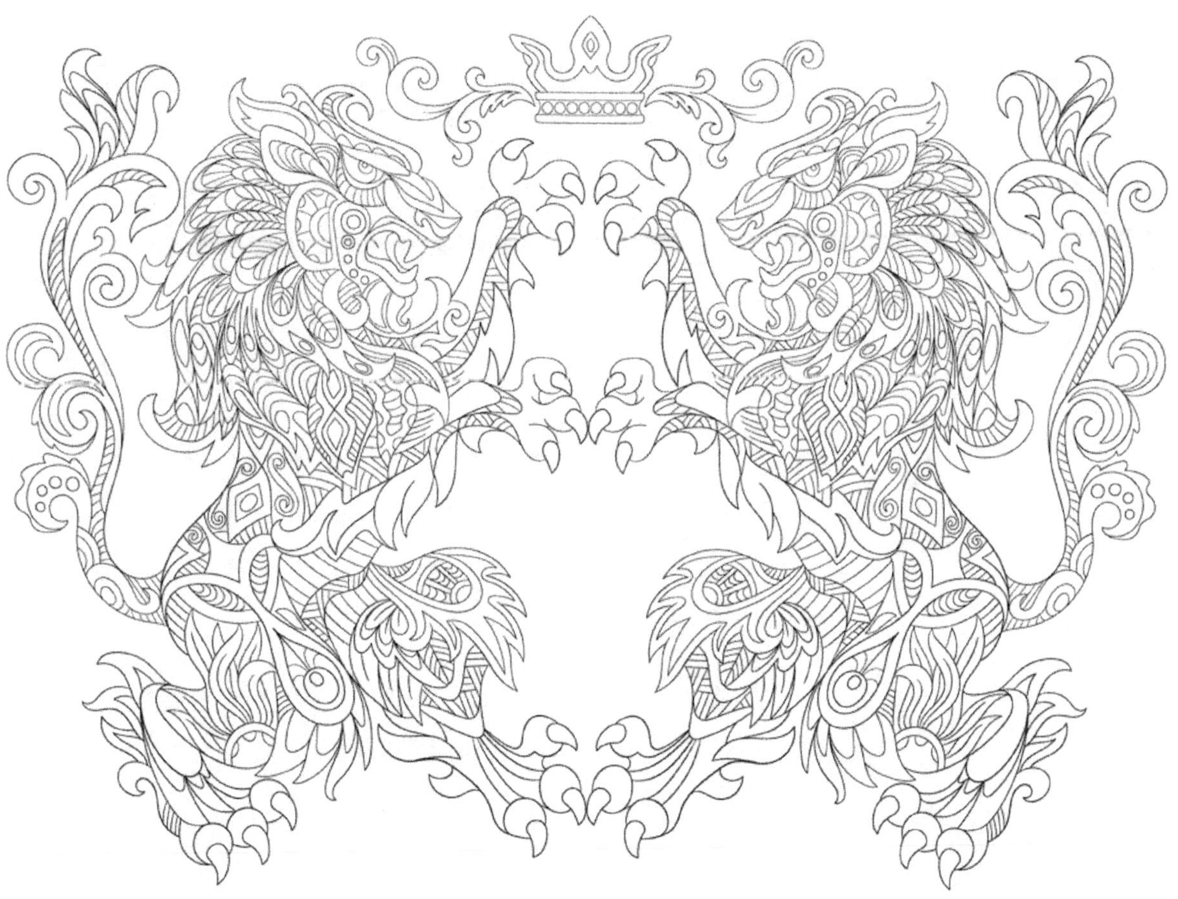

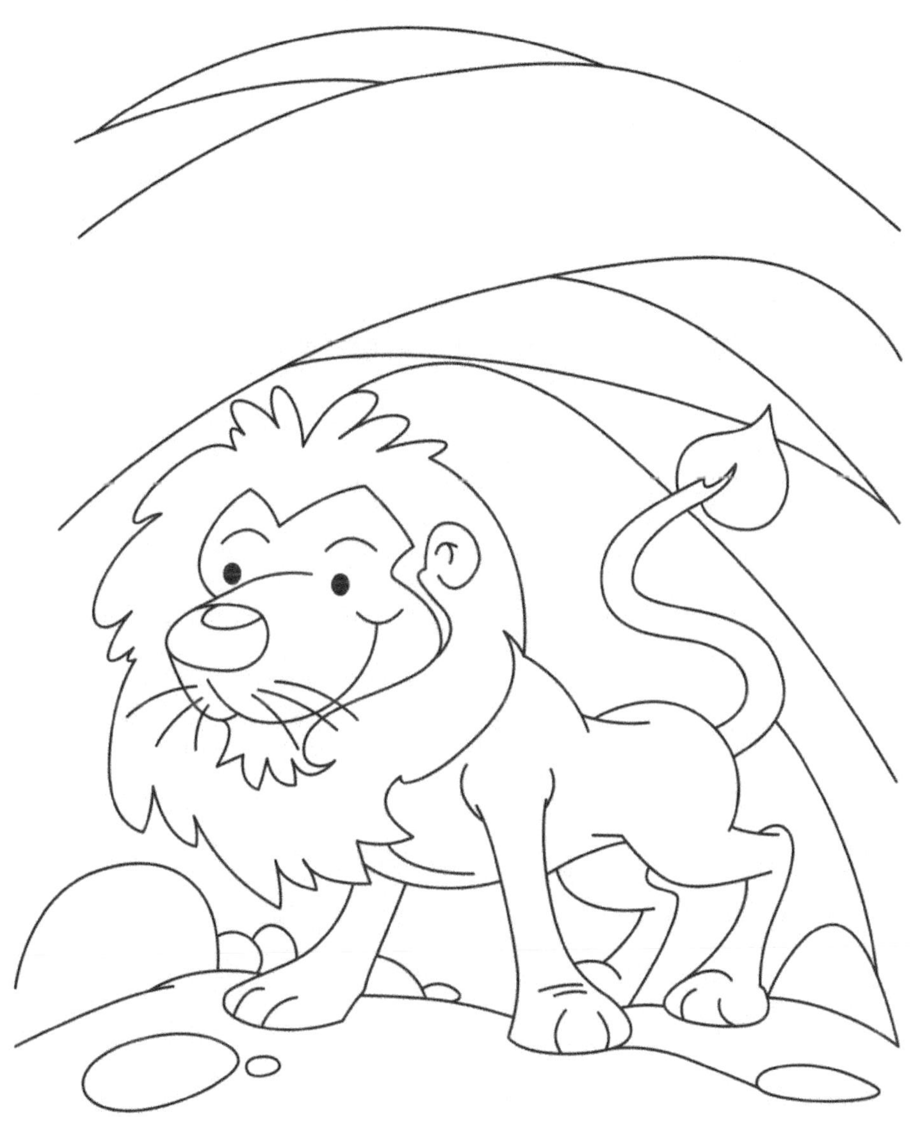

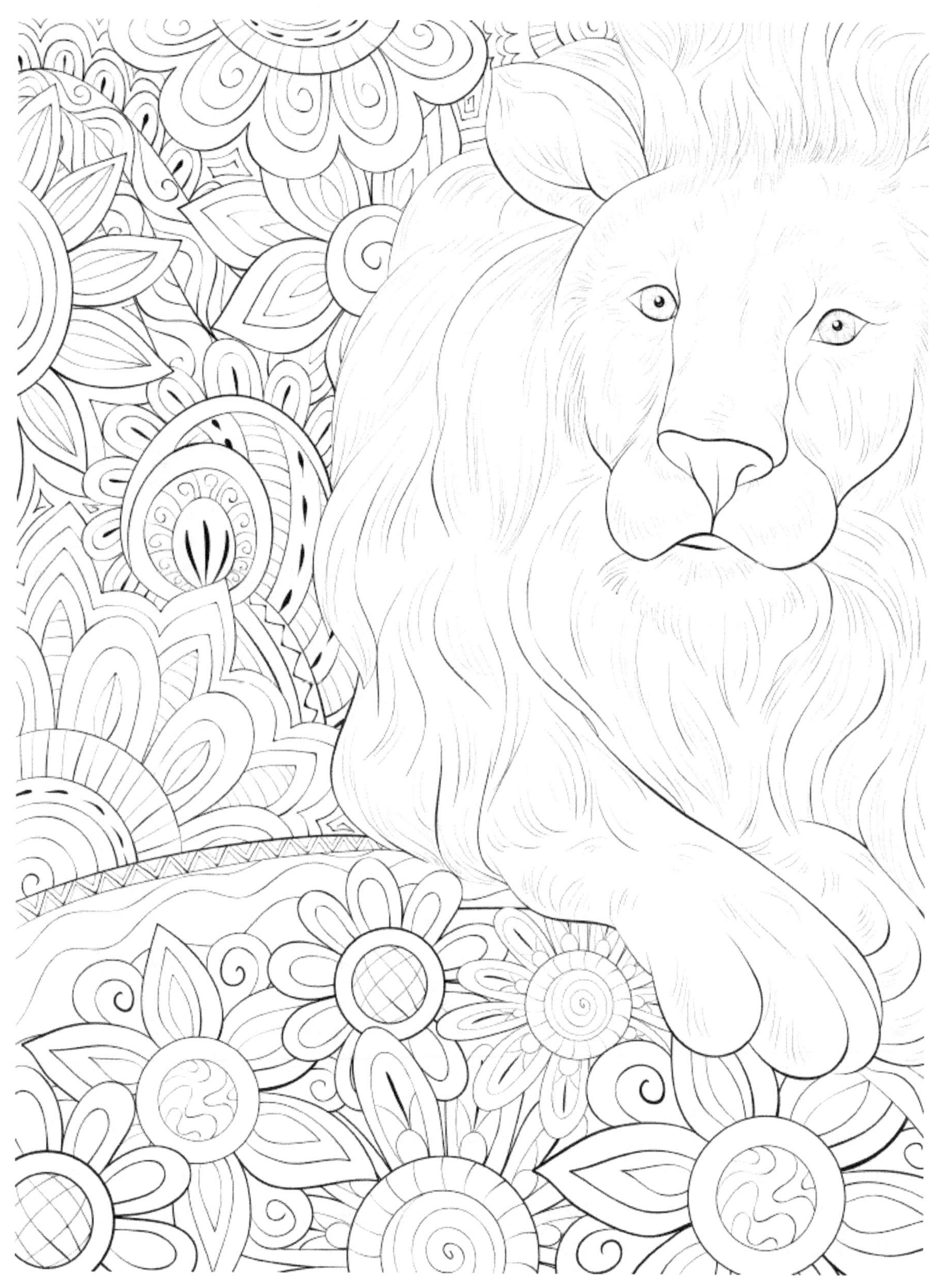

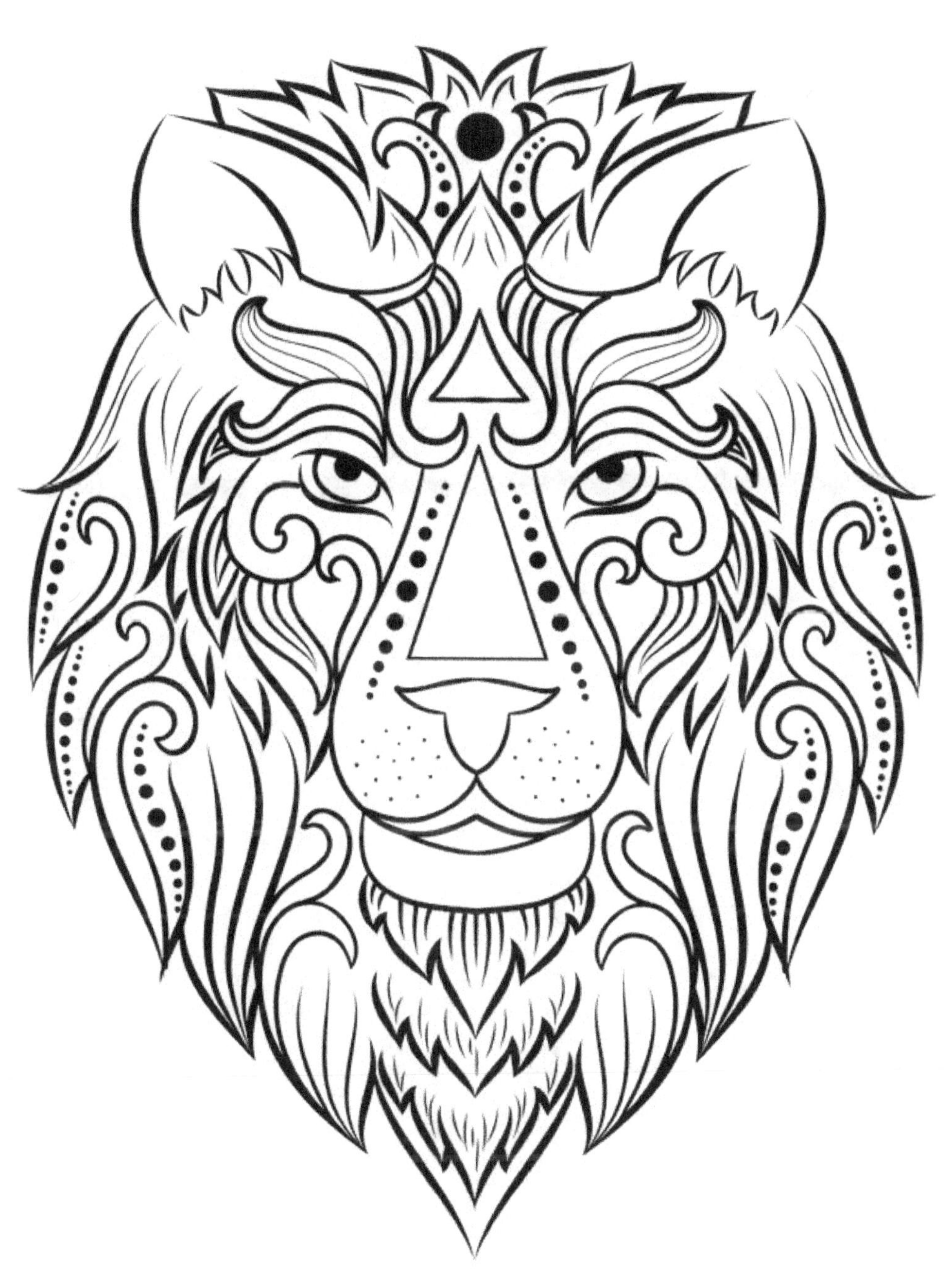

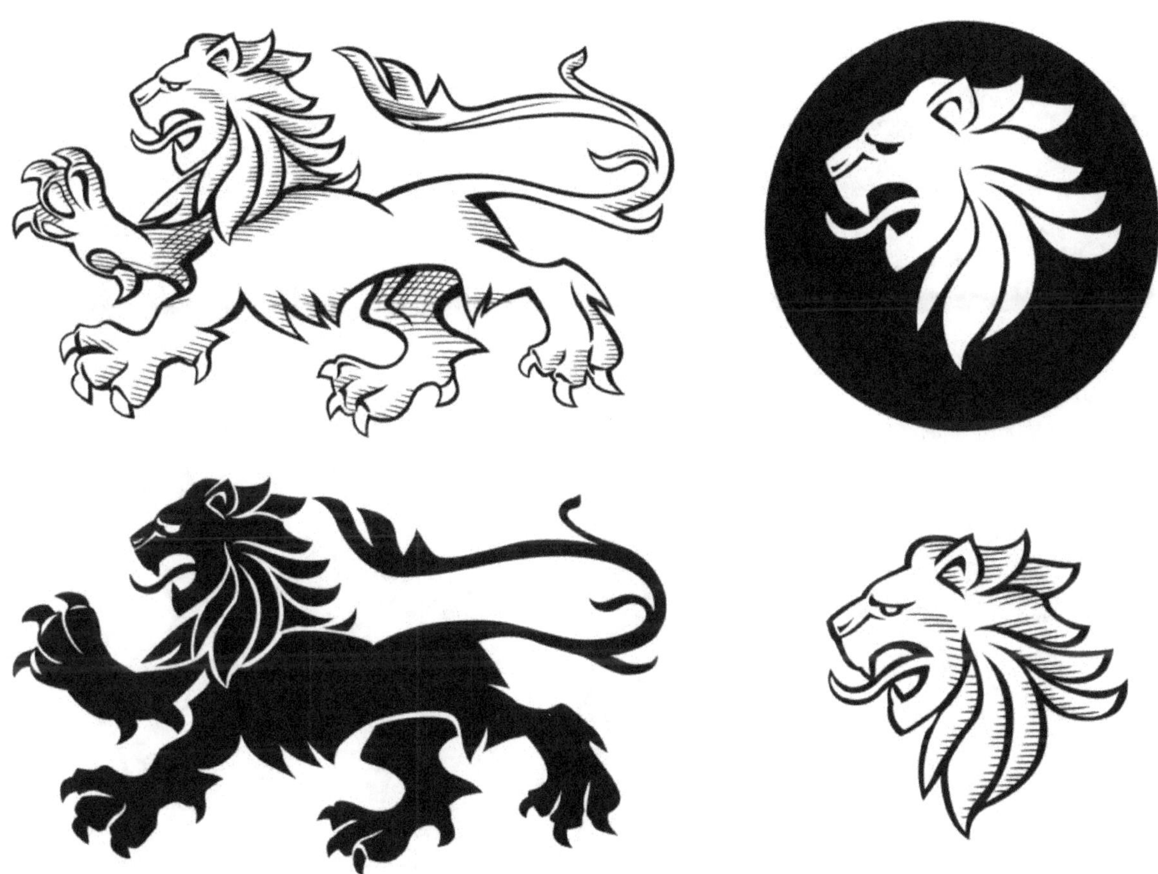

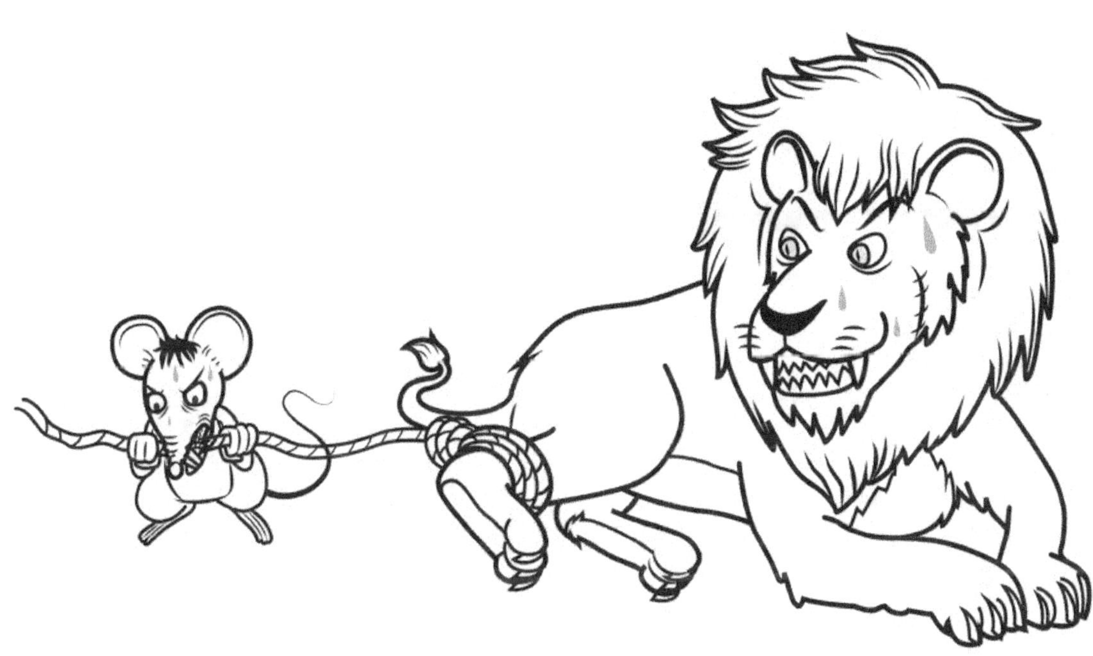

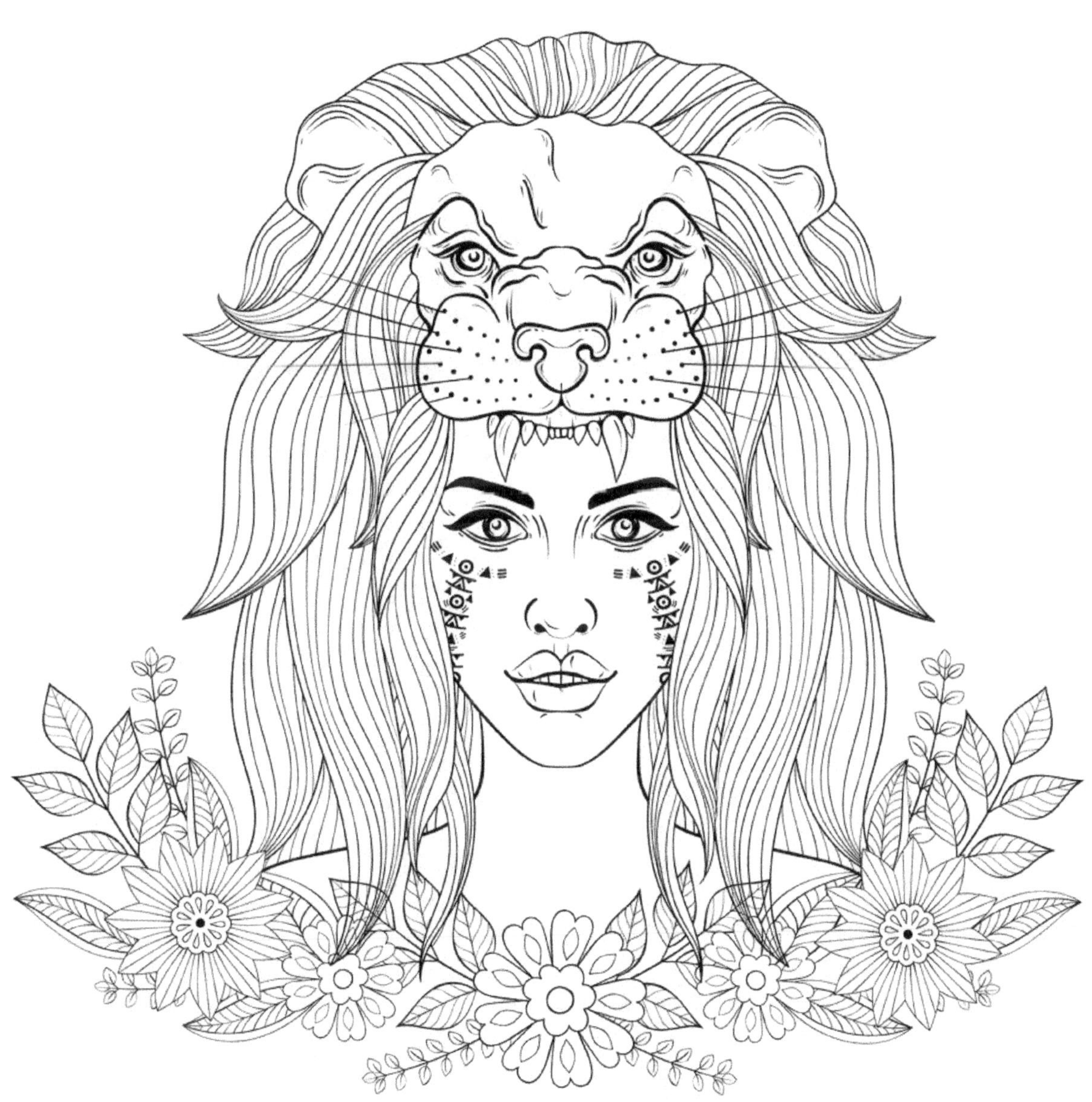

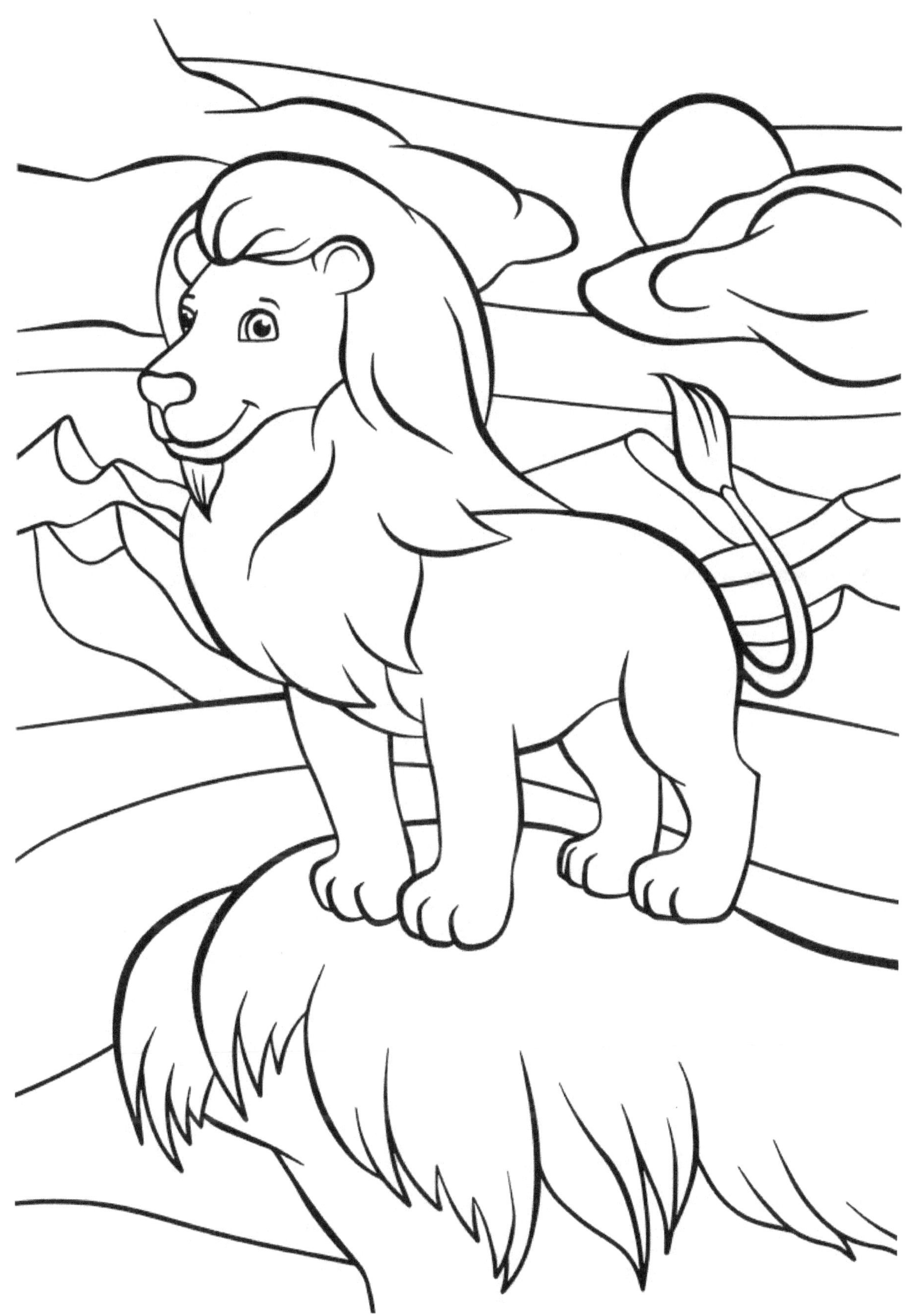

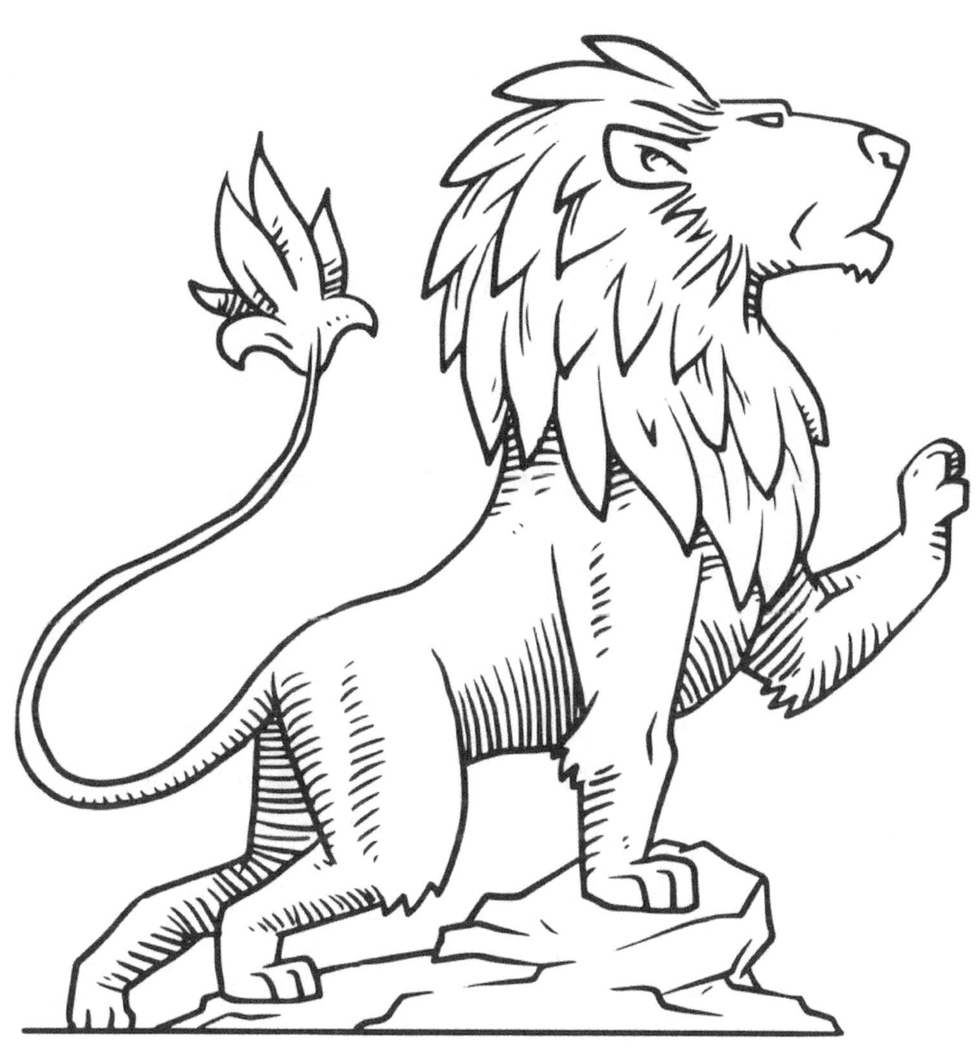

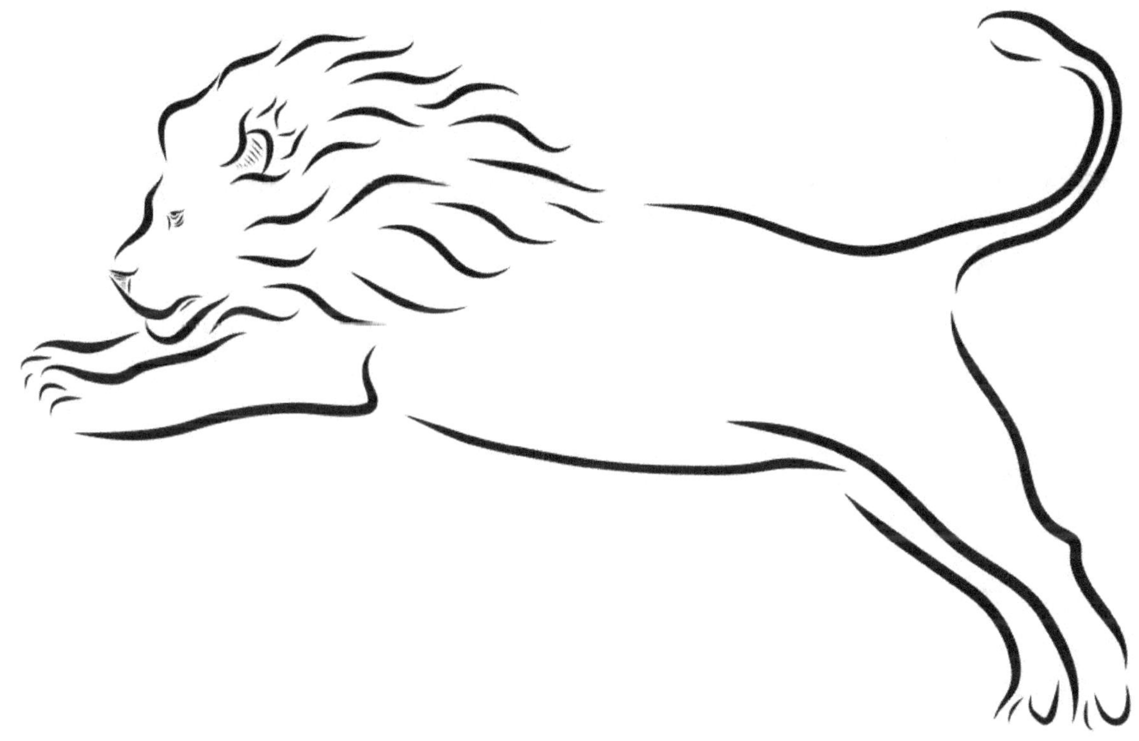

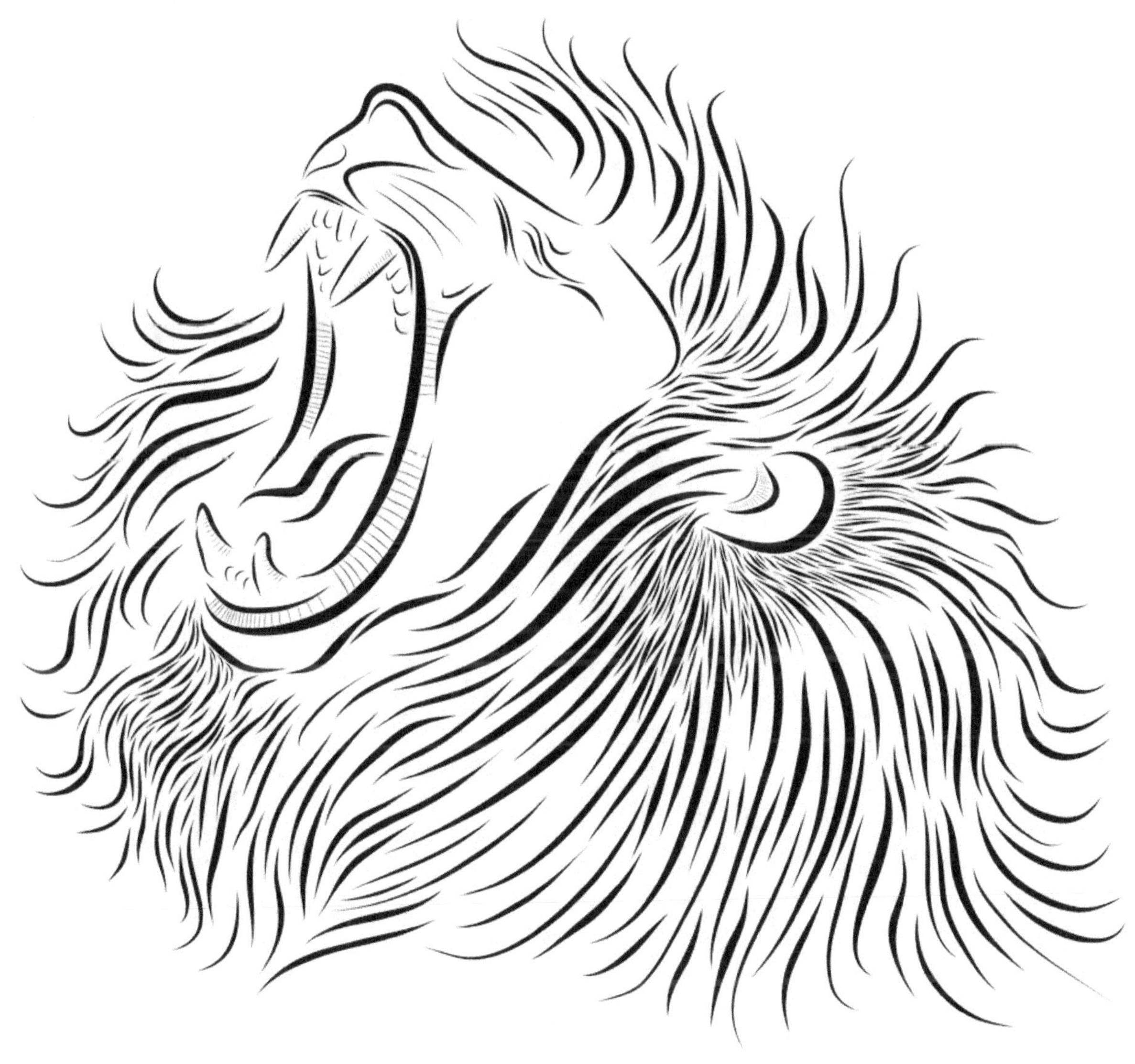